Caring Through Cancer

By

Suzanna Stokes

and

Lara Woodward

Copyright © 2018
Suzanna Stokes and Lara Woodward

This Book is dedicated in

memory of our Husbands

Contents

1.	Introduction	1
2.	Life Before Cancer	6
3.	The Beginning	9
4.	Passing on the News	23
5.	Work	27
6.	The Treatment Plan	32
7.	Chemotherapy	38
8.	Surgery	49
9.	Radiotherapy	54
10.	Infection	58
11.	Scans	61
12.	Medication	66
13.	Out of Hours	72
14.	Visiting Hospital	79
15.	Managing at Home During Treatment	83
16.	Food	87
17.	From Spouse to Carer	94
18.	Support	99
19.	Macmillan Online Community	102
20.	Moods	108
21.	Fears and Worries	113
22.	The Loving Relationship	116
23.	Family and Friends	119
24.	Last Holiday	126
25.	Last Chance	129
26.	Counselling	131
27.	When the Cancer is Incurable	138
28.	The End Stages of Life	144
29.	At the Hospice	152
30.	Feelings after Death	161
31.	Grief	165
32.	Moving on	171
33.	The Circle of Life	179
34.	Epilogue – Meeting Each Other	181

Introduction

This book is about our personal experiences of caring for a loved one with incurable cancer. For us it was our husbands. We have tried to be open about how we felt, what we went through and what we learnt.

We are very aware and would like to acknowledge that other carers will have their own range of unique experiences and emotions as hard, or harder, than our own.

We are also aware there are carers who are more isolated than we were, may have significant financial worries, difficulties with their families or their employers and those who may be trying to raise a young family, or look after elderly parents, while holding down a job at the same time. For many carers cancer is not the only traumatic or stressful situation in their lives. We wish more help and support was available for these carers than currently appears to be the case.

To protect family and friends, names have been changed and place names withheld. For the same reason parts of our stories will remain untold.

Suzanna's First Thoughts

When I started to write about my journey as a carer, I had no idea how far I would get with it, or if I would even complete the project. I had made notes throughout Mark's illness, as a sort of diary of events, with the vague idea of writing a book at some point, mainly as a journal for our family to look back on. It felt good to get words on paper, a sort of release and very therapeutic.

But once I teamed up with a very good friend from the Macmillan site, I suddenly felt inspired, this was meant to be. I was urged on by our team work, together we could and would achieve our goal. We got on so well together and finally I had someone to compare notes, check writing and share ideas with. I was delighted!

Suddenly it all became more real and more possible to achieve. I felt a certain determination to succeed, for our hubbies, families, for us and all the carers out there doing an amazing job, day in day out. The unsung heroes.

We thought how helpful it could be for people new to caring to get two honest and open versions of events, two carers view of the enormity of it all; the responsibility, frustrations, loneliness and the struggle to carry on with the physical and emotional affect it has on you. But also the rewards and human side of caring for someone you love.

There are others the book may help or who may benefit from reading it. Medical staff, family and friends, to get a view of how it really feels, from the other side of the fence, to care for someone with cancer, especially incurable cancer.

For me writing seems to come more easily in the middle of the night. Awkward and inconvenient, yes, but I just wake up with a head full of ideas and inspiration. I get up, grab for a pen and paper, and off I go. As I scribble away, the thoughts in my head appear on the paper and empty my overflowing mind.

I am hoping, eventually, we will produce a book that is not the norm. A book written from carers to carers, that is informative, empathetic, and inevitably sometimes very sad, but hopefully valuable and worthwhile. We will tell it truthfully; how it felt for us, our hubbies and families, who we turned to, how we coped and the ups and downs, all laid out in a sequence of events.

I was not in any way, shape or form ready to lose my wonderful husband. Nor was he anywhere near ready to lose his life. He was 58 years old and very much looking forward to retiring at 60. After 35 years of working permanent night shifts, he felt he had done his share on the work front. So we decided I would retire too and we would spend quality time together, while we were still fit and able to do so.

We had decided we would buy a cosy little caravan down by the seaside somewhere and just potter up and down to it. Keeping the house on as a winter base and lending the van to friends and family for short breaks. We wanted to take the grandchildren down with us in the school holidays, coming home to visit family and do essential maintenance jobs to the house and garden. It would be a time to generally slow down, relax and enjoy life and we were very happy with our plan. After years of Mark not seeing daylight, finally a much needed reward. Or so we thought.

Sadly this was not to be, as he became desperately ill. Little did we know then that this was to be the beginning of his precious life being snatched away, way too soon and our whole lives were about to be turned upside down. All our wonderful plans of a long and happy retirement, snuffed out like a candle. Puff, gone. Mark would never see his retirement years, or his hard worked for pension. We would never get our quality time together either, we were heartbroken but we were in this together.

Lara's First Thoughts

It seems more and more people are surviving certain types cancer, or living longer with it. Cancer treatments continue to improve and hopefully their side effects will be less aggressive in the future. Five family members and friends have had the disease. Three are living and two have not. That is better than the odds even a few years ago. Although more people are being diagnosed with cancer more of them are living for longer with the disease and my husband was one of those. I am grateful for that extra time.

Caring for a spouse, partner, or a loved one with cancer is incredibly tough whether that cancer is curable or incurable. It takes over your life and you can feel isolated and lonely with no-one to turn to who fully understands quite what you are having to go through, day after day.

When Suzanna suggested writing a book I was so unsure about it. Me? A book? What did I have to offer anyone? But then I realised Suzanna and I had what carers may find invaluable, we had experiences we could share and we had understanding of what it could be like. If one carer, or a concerned friend or family member who found it hard to understand, could feel helped by reading our stories maybe it was worth it.

And, it has to be said, Suzanna is mighty persuasive! We "met" on the Macmillan support forum and we struck up a friendship that has continued. Suzanna helped me through some of the toughest patches and lowest periods during my time as a carer. We shared the ups and downs with understanding and quite a few jokes. She is full of common sense, has a great sense of humour and is one of the kindest people that, at the time of writing this, I have never actually had the pleasure of meeting.

That will change, this year I hope, and we will sit down and drink tea and eat cake (lemon drizzle) and walk in the woods and laugh, probably shed a tear or two, and then work on this little book of ours. For now we write, offer each other advice and suggestions about what can be added or changed, and then we put our words together. Suzanna is much more disciplined than I am with her writing but she is also a great prompter.   As our husbands' cancer type and treatments were different, between us what we went through covers many of things that a carer may experience.

Nick was 47 when he was diagnosed and 52 when he died. He didn't have a high risk profile and he didn't have a bad bone in his body. He was a good person, an incredible person and we were so proud of him and all he achieved in life. Although those five years were some of the hardest years of my life, there were also good times.   I wouldn't have let anyone else care for Nick and it was an honour to be able to give him the support he needed when he needed it most, to be there for him. Love is about give and take and knowing when to do which.

Life before Cancer

Suzanna

I was just 15 years old and working as an apprentice hairdresser, with his twin Sister, when I first set eyes on Mark. He was very handsome and I was instantly attracted to him. Sadly the feeling wasn't mutual, and when his Sister mentioned me to him later that day, he replied, "She is just a kid!" As he was two years older than me, I must have seemed very young to him at the time. He was working as an engineer at a factory nearby and he finished his shift before we shut.

Time passed by, with him occasionally popping into the shop, to get the house key from his sister, who delighted in embarrassing us both, by saying " No key until you say hello to Suzanna". Being quiet and shy I felt exposed, but as he mumbled hello, I could see he was equally embarrassed about it and that just made me like him even more.

Once I was 17, I had my long hair cut short and started to wear a little makeup and one day after Mark had been to the shop he asked his Sister who the new girl was. She replied, "That's Suzanna!" to which came the response "wow she's grown up!" The rest is history. He asked me out, we got engaged when I was 18, and married when I was 20.

Despite lots of ups and downs along the way we were happy. We lost all of our parents over time. Also, sadly, a baby who was born with heart defects. But it didn't break us, in fact it brought us closer together. We had three other sons and some turbulent teenage years with them, but we carried on regardless. Mark was placid and I was a stress machine, somehow it balanced out. He knew how to calm me down like no one else did, I could pour out all my worries to him and he would listen to me and fix what he could. It worked well for us, we were right for each other and as the years moved on we became secure in our own world and were very comfortable in each other's company.

Lara

It was during my first week of student life and I was at a fresher's dance in a night club when I noticed a boy walking across the dance floor in his biking leathers. He had a crash helmet under his arm and his black hair was shining under the disco ball reflections. That was it, I was head over heels. Nick had the biggest darkest eyes and huge but gentle hands, a soft voice and a good, kind heart. He also had huge intelligence and a willingness to share it with others, which is how I ended up getting to know him better. When I was struggling with one of the modules on my course he helped me and gave me the confidence I needed to understand the subject.

By the end of the first term we were inseparable and remained together until we completed our degrees. Motor bike became a beaten up old car, he went on to do a post grad course and I started working but still we stayed committed to each other alternating our weekends between his student flat and my city flat some hours away. Nick graduated and went to work abroad, meaning we saw each other only once a year but still there was no one else for either of us and so, after three years, I went to join him. Those were great days.

We married, had children, and shared our lives. Back in the UK he worked long hours and travelled a lot. Our children and

I missed him when he was away and loved the time we were all together. I kept busy being a mum and working for a local charity. Yes, there were ups and downs, a lifelong relationship requires compromise and effort, but we were happy and I felt blessed. I accepted that his job gave him pleasure and was hugely important to him. But I knew that when he retired, or went part time (I wasn't convinced he would ever retire), we would be able to enjoy plenty of time together again, travelling, exploring, learning and just being us. Life was good and uncomplicated. But all that was about to change when we found out, after sharing more than half a lifetime, we weren't going to grow old together.

The Beginning – Diagnosis and Prognosis

The start of living alongside cancer, as a spouse or partner and carer, was more than being thrown in at the deep end, it was being in a kayak on a fast flowing river without a paddle. As the journey progresses the adrenalin continues to pump as you face the changing currents and the hidden rocks just below the surface. You learn a lot about yourself in a short time, face fear and despair, find energy and drive when you thought you had none left and find courage that you didn't know you had.

Both of us had a different start to our Cancer journeys but both, sadly, involved delayed diagnosis. One of us had a husband who was outwardly very ill, the other a husband who had only one obvious symptom but otherwise appeared relatively well. One of them was treated by the NHS the other a combination of privately and the NHS as he had a company health care plan, one of us had a Macmillan nurse the other not. So, differences but still both of us caring for our husbands who had an incurable disease. Here is where our stories started.

Suzanna

Mark started to feel ill with sciatica in September 2013. After being signed off work for two weeks and a prescription for strong painkillers he returned to his job but was still feeling unwell. Then he began to have severe and continual headaches that were not relieved with pain killers. He couldn't bear any noise or light and started to wear sunglasses continually.

Back to the doctors he went and was sent for a brain scan.

This showed no abnormalities, so gave no apparent reason for the headaches. Without any explanation of why he was suffering, he was just given stronger painkillers. Next he started to have angina attacks and, as he had already had a stent fitted seven years earlier, they rechecked his heart with an echo scan. Again nothing was found to be wrong.

By Christmas Mark was desperately ill, with visits to hospital both Christmas Eve and New Year's Eve, which once again provided no answers. He was put on steroids to try and ease the awful headaches. There was no improvement, he was rapidly losing weight and looked an awful colour.

The neighbours started to ask what was wrong with Mark, one even said "Does he have cancer?" to which I replied "Not as far as we know." though deep down I felt sure he did and I was worried sick. But, with no diagnosis, what else could I possibly say? I felt he definitely had cancer somewhere in his body, but had no idea where. We were determined to keep visiting hospital until they found it.

Into the New Year and his sick notes were now saying temporal arteritis which, although incorrect, was at least an improvement on ' generally unwell '. His employers were getting impatient by this stage and asked him to attend a meeting for a medical update with them. He was so ill he could hardly climb the stairs to the office. Mark looked absolutely dreadful and I think they were shocked when they saw him.

At Hospital a full CAT scan was requested, but we heard nothing and continually tried to chase it up. He was referred to the Rheumatology department, but they were unable to make a diagnosis either. The consultant could see there was something very wrong with him, he looked so awful. A chest x-ray had shown slight changes but she said there was no sign of lung cancer (thank god!). We told her we were still waiting for the full CAT scan, so she rang down to the x-ray department to chase it up and was told they hadn't received a request for one. That felt absolutely awful, as if they had dismissed the urgency and the importance of Mark's illness and suffering. She ordered one as a matter of priority and said if this found nothing wrong, he would be referred to the Neurology department.

The appointment arrived and I went with Mark. He was injected with dye and finally given a CAT scan. By now it was the end of February, almost six months since he first felt unwell.

Before long we had a phone call from the Hospital with an appointment at the outpatient clinic. Our minds were racing, how come they had contacted us so quickly? There must be something terribly wrong, they must have found something. As the whole family held their breaths we went to the appointment and finally they had something to tell us….

We sat facing a Macmillan Nurse Consultant, although we were totally unaware of that at the time, nothing about her would suggest so, no uniform or name badge. She was in a small office, with an examination couch, sink, and a desk with a computer and screen. After giving Mark a thorough examination, she pulled up two chairs for us and sat at her desk.

Looking at Mark she said "we have the results of your CAT scan… ", pulling the image onto the screen came the bombshell, "….you have advanced Lung Cancer ". Everything was said very gently and in a matter of fact way, she kept her tone level and calm. Even so the words bounced around my head over and over again, it sounded like my head was in a bucket, as her voice echoed. Lung Cancer!

I felt as if someone had just dropped a house brick on my chest, it felt heavy and took my breath. I remember pulling at hand towels from above her sink. But the tears stayed in my eyes stinging and sticking, burning. Her small office suddenly became much smaller and claustrophobic, I wanted to get out. NO! This couldn't be true! I felt physically sick.

Looking at Mark he appeared frozen to the spot, statue like, showing no type of emotion at all. He seemed stunned, probably in shock. Everything else she said was muffled and distant as my mind raced away into the future and all we had to face ahead of us. While she continued to talk I struggled to stay focused. I was aware that it was important to listen to what she was saying, but it was so difficult.

"He will need biopsies to determine exactly which type of Lung Cancer we are dealing with" she said. TYPES? I didn't know there were types! To me Lung Cancer was Lung Cancer, plain and simple. Obviously I had a lot to learn. We were then told it was incurable and inoperable so any treatment would be palliative, to shrink tumours and to prolong his life, not to cure him.

Once the biopsy results were back we would see an Oncologist, with a view to arranging any treatment on offer. The screen on her desk still displayed an image of his scan. There was a large tumour in his right lung and mets (metastases or secondary tumours), which had travelled to his other lung, pleural lining and liver, a truly horrendous sight.

She asked if we were okay for money and gave us a card for Macmillan CAB to get advice and support and to claim any benefits we were entitled to. After being given a prescription for morphine to help with the pain we were sent to the pharmacy. This was where the enormity of it all sank in and we both sobbed uncontrollably.

Mark needed a bronchoscopy and had it done in the Day Case Unit. It's a very unpleasant procedure, but was totally necessary to diagnose which type of cancer he had. Our newly assigned Macmillan nurse met us on the ward. She held our hands and asked if we were okay and if Mark had taken his morphine. He hadn't wanted to start relying on it yet but we were told he must start taking it, he would need it. Also the doctor who was going to carry out the procedure came out, introduced himself to Mark and shook his hand which I thought was a lovely gesture.

When Mark was wheeled away to have the procedure he looked so ill and I was worried it would knock him about. I went to get a drink in the cafe and wait for him feeling very anxious and with a deep sense of impending doom. I knew the news wouldn't be good and wondered what they could possibly do to make things any better.

After the procedure had been done they told Mark that they'd found lots of nodules in his gullet which was not a good sign. The fact his voice was hoarse was apparently another alarm bell. The biopsies were very painful and uncomfortable but it had been done now, so he could go home and rest. He looked incredibly pale and tired and I just wanted to hug him and make it all go away.

Back at home he wasn't at all well, his breathing became laboured and his voice became even more hoarse. He looked ashen and kept wanting to go into the garden to get some fresh air, or open the window and lean out. It seemed the procedure had caused bleeding in the lungs which we were unaware of, and life threatening blood clots were very slowly building up.

Back at hospital for the biopsy results the same Macmillan nurse consultant saw us again. She told us that his cancer was none small cell adenocarcinoma and that he would be sent an appointment with an oncologist shortly to discuss treatment options. Little did we know, before that could happen, he would collapse and be rushed into hospital.

Soon after the appointment Mark collapsed in the middle of the night, gasping for breath and was rushed into Hospital by ambulance. I was waiting outside the resuscitation room all night while they struggled to stabilise him. Feeling panicky, lost and alone, I rang his twin sister as I was not coping at all well. She came straight to the Hospital along with her husband. We sat through the night waiting for news, I can remember pacing and that the drink machine wasn't working, otherwise it was all very much of a blur. The next day he was moved to the coronary care unit with two pulmonary embolisms and we were told he may not last the day out. Family were sent for and we were all ushered into a relatives' room.

Then came our Macmillan nurse, like a ray of sunshine on your darkest day. She took care of the whole family which was no mean task. Our youngest son had run off into the car park panicking and our middle Son insisted they resuscitate Mark should the worst happen, against medical advice and my wishes. They explained that his blood had been thinned so drastically that he would just bleed out everywhere, should they try to resuscitate him, leaving him with unnecessary suffering and maybe brain damage. He would have hated that. The nurse was wonderful, calm, patient and very caring. She stayed by our sides for a whole week as Mark battled on, determined not to give in. We will never forget her kindness, compassion and her talent for 'just being there' when she was needed most.

Mark did pull through, against all the odds, with sheer grit and determination. Before he came home our Mac nurse sorted everything out for us, from medication, oxygen, benefits, disabled badge, counselling and a wheelchair, to Community Mac nurse and district nurses. Mark's cancer was incurable, but she did everything possible to make whatever time he had left comfortable. A truly inspirational young woman and a credit to her profession. We have remained friends.

At the point of diagnosis I guess I was incredibly angry, shocked and upset. Mark had been through so much and I wanted answers to my questions. As time passed by I calmed down. I'm not a bitter or resentful person and I tried to answer some of these questions myself. I always like to be fair and see the other person's point of view, otherwise you end up with a one sided story. I never wanted to make anyone look bad, I just needed to put all of the niggling doubts to bed and move on. There were so many questions and I tried to find answers for all of them.

I asked our GP why it had taken so long to diagnose lung cancer? She said lung cancer is a difficult one, as it may start in the centre of the lung and grow outwards. Therefore not causing any symptoms until it hits the outer walls. This answer satisfied me and I was then able to put it to bed.

I asked why the cancer wasn't found by the hospital much earlier. Why was the only treatment offered more and more painkillers therefore escalating the medication instead of finding the cause? If a patient presents with a continual, severe headache logic tells you to look at his head, which they did. If he then presents with angina, logic tells you to look at his heart, which again they did. Mark's illness was classed as non-urgent, as nothing had been found seriously wrong so far.

I wanted to know why we were told there was no sign of lung cancer on the x-ray when the cancer was so significant? As Mark was so ill a chest x-ray was done as a routine check but it didn't pick up the cancer as the image was so grainy, only showing abnormally large veins.

Why was the cancer left to spread through his body while they tried to work out what was wrong? Mark was misdiagnosed with temporal arteritis, so the doctors weren't looking for anything else at the time, they thought they knew what was wrong.

Why, when he had a constant headache, was breathless and had a strange throat rattle at night, did they not suspect lung cancer? If you google these symptoms, it clearly says that could be the cause. Well, they tell you to never google symptoms as it can scare you, but in this instance it was correct. I did actually google it, but perished the thought of cancer at the time.
Why did the Hospital say his tests weren't urgent, as in an amber light, instead of a red light, leaving him to suffer? Was it because they had absolutely no idea he had cancer? Had they ruled out any urgent diagnosis and were they looking for something less serious?

Why was his cat scan not booked when it should have been? I believe there was absolutely no answer or excuse here, it was obviously Hospital error.

One more question I kept asking myself was why was Mark not given a full CAT scan at the onset? He had a head scan, an echo heart scan and then finally a CAT scan as it was needed anyway. This only wasted time and money, probably allowing the cancer to spread and multiply away, while they looked for other complaints and leaving it way too late to do anything that may have saved his life or at least given him longer.

Lara's Story

Nick's cancer went undiagnosed for too long. He went to the GP in 2008 as he had noticed blood in his stools and was sent for a colonoscopy where "nothing significant" was found. He was told it was probably haemorrhoids and not to worry but he did worry as he had never had a problem with his bowels before. Two years later, during which time Nick had repeatedly visited the GP with his concerns, only to be told he was healthy and to stop worrying, he asked for a second opinion. The GP reluctantly agreed but not without saying it would be a waste of time, and he was at last given another colonoscopy. The only tangible symptom during those two years was the presence of blood. He had also started feeling tired and looking drawn, but then he had a busy job, travelled abroad often, and worked extremely long hours so that wasn't entirely unexpected.

I picked Nick up from the hospital after the repeat colonoscopy and drove him home. He was chatting but not quite himself, on edge, which I put down to the medication he'd been given for the procedure. When we arrived home he sat me on the sofa next to him, gently took my hand and simply said "Lara, I've got cancer". Apparently he had been advised not to tell me until we got home so my driving wasn't affected by the news.

Cancer had entered my life nearly two years earlier when a dear friend had been diagnosed with brain cancer. I couldn't believe it was happening again. The shock seemed to prevent an emotional outburst and sent me into practical mode. I had questions, lots of them, but of course Nick didn't have the answers yet. All he knew was that they had found cancer, the consultant said he thought it was early stage but he would need a full scan and the biopsy results first.   Early stage, well that at least sounded positive, bowel cancer was treatable.

The GP was shocked and even apologised. We hoped that this experience would mean that in future she would take a patient seriously if they had concerns about their health even if they didn't fit the "norm" for a cancer sufferer. I was angrier than Nick, especially with the hospital doctor that carried out the first colonoscopy and probably missed the cancer when it would most likely have been less advanced. He just said doctors are human and make mistakes but if he could help stop someone else suffering the same way that would be good so he made sure the original doctor knew the situation. It had been suggested that, first time round, the procedure may have been carried out incorrectly, starting too high in the colon and so missing the tumour which was very low down.

The first lesson I learnt about living alongside cancer is that things don't happen as quickly as you want them to. There is a lot of frustrating, infuriating, terrifying waiting to be done. When eventually the requested body scan was carried out we went off to the hospital for the news. It wasn't good and it was told to us bluntly, without compassion or care, but I suppose there is no easy way to hear news like that. In the two years since the first colonoscopy the colorectal cancer had developed to stage four with extensive spread to both of Nick's lungs and his liver. The primary tumour was very large and inoperable.

Again shock. We knew there was cancer, that there would be treatment but to sit there and be told my husband had stage four incurable cancer, that was inoperable, just rendered me speechless. I couldn't think, I couldn't cry, I couldn't even feel angry at that moment, I was having a hard enough time just remembering to breathe. Nick was outwardly in control though goodness knows what he was feeling inside, he was never one to share his feelings without a bit of a prod. No tears, just calm logical processing of the information as was his way. The doctor explained Nick would be put under an oncologist and they would "see what they could do".

In that one short appointment our lives were turned upside down, inside out and changed for good. We went from a family with hardly a care in the world, living a good and largely happy life, to a family who had a dangerous and unwelcome interloper living with us, feeding off Nick and getting ready to pull us all down. Nick was a non-smoker, slim, healthy eating, 47 year old who rarely drank, ran 5 days a week and did Pilates regularly. How could he have incurable cancer? How?

Our first appointment with Nick's oncologist was like a badly needed burst of sunshine on a dark day. He was direct about the extent of Nick's cancer but also said that he was young and fit. After talking though what Nick wanted he said they would throw the full works at him in terms of treatment. It would be aggressive but the cancer was so extensive that would be the best option to give him more time. Goodness, how we wanted as much time as we could have.

We never received a prognosis in terms of time scales, Nick was clear he didn't want one, but the first doctor had made comments that made us think months rather than years. At least the oncologist gave us some hope there. Prognosis in cancer seems to be little more than an educated guess based on the stage and spread of the cancer, the type and the statistics plus the general health and age of the person with the disease. It, of course, can also change over time. I know people who have lived far shorter than their original prognosis and others, including Nick and my friend, who have beaten the odds. As always with cancer different people want to deal with things in different ways. For me, for us, we didn't want to be mentally ticking days off a calendar waiting for that final day to arrive so we joined the "one day at a time" brigade and stayed on it the best we could for as long as we could.

There were more delays before the final treatment plan was decided. More tests, on the functioning of Nick's major organs to determine that he was fit enough for the treatment being planned. Thankfully, despite the spread of the cancer, everything was working well and the treatment was planned, and approved. He would be started on chemotherapy as the primary tumour was inoperable and radiotherapy could only target one area which would leave all the mets, the secondary tumours in his liver and lungs, untreated.

Things we learnt

- Cancer can be hard to diagnose and mistakes can be made. Don't be afraid to ask for a second opinion or to ask questions if a diagnosis for symptoms seems to be taking a long time.

- Listen to the patient. If this is a person who rarely goes to the doctors, then suddenly keeps returning week after week feeling incredibly ill, losing weight and looking dreadful they should be taken seriously and investigated fully.
- Not every cancer sufferer fits the stereotype.
- Doing some research can be useful but bear in mind that there is inaccurate and out of date information on the internet. We used to stick to well respected sites such as Cancer Research UK. Macmillan and some of the specialist cancer charity sites, where the information is up to date, accurate and reviewed on a regular basis. Bear in mind that what you google isn't necessarily fact or evidence of a disease, it may just indicate the need to investigate symptoms further.
- There is no good or easy way to hear that someone has cancer. You can be told gently or quite bluntly, whichever way the news hits hard.
- Expect to wait. For scans, for appointments, for other tests and follow up appointments before treatment even begins.
- It can be hard to remember everything that is said or discussed at an appointment. Maybe take a pen and paper or a way of making a few notes with you. We often found that two heads were better than one and it was something the carer could do that felt useful.
- If you have questions then write them and take them with you, it is so easy to forget things. Ask other questions as you think of them.
- Try and find out when the follow up appointment will be or what the next stage is. It can help to always know what is happening next.

- No prognosis is written in stone.
- Devising a treatment plan can take time. It is worth the wait if it means that your loved one will get the very best treatment available.
- Ask any questions you want answered now, don't be afraid to query anything you are unsure or unhappy about. Treatment is a major decision, you will need to be 100% happy with it, and rest assured you did what was right for you.

Passing on the news

Suzanna

Once we had a firm Lung Cancer diagnosis, we informed people in strict priority order. That being our Sons first and all three were informed simultaneously. Our Sons and partners all came straight round to the house that evening, visibly shaken and deeply upset by the news. They wanted to see their Dad and were struggling to digest the enormity of his prognosis. They hoped to discuss how to prolong his life, but as we had no treatment plan yet it wasn't possible. They were understandably impatient for answers, but they were answers that we just couldn't provide at that time. We would have a wait for a treatment plan.

Then we told Mark's twin sister, followed by my two sisters and my brother, plus some very close friends. Those people knew we were at the Hospital for results, so were already waiting for news. Breaking the news to these people was both difficult and heart breaking, but they deserved to hear it from us and not via someone else.

Work came next and that was difficult, especially Mark's work, as the penny then dropped that he would never go back there. But they were very understanding, as were my work colleagues. Hubby did not wish to discuss his illness, so no big announcements, nothing on social media, he was a very private man. In fact there was nothing on social media throughout his illness, it was never mentioned on there at all until after his death, it was his choice, his illness, his decision. There was no big rush to tell other people. It had been apparent for some time just how ill Mark was, so keeping it a secret was not an option. In fact some people had already guessed he had cancer, just by looking at him and as is always the case, bad news travels fast. Neighbours witnessed constant visits from Nurses and realised how serious it was. Eventually most people were aware of Hubby's illness, but even after his death a few people didn't even know he was ill. It is impossible to track everyone you know down.

When treatment started, I found it easier to pass on news via a general text to everyone, on a need to know basis. The constant phone calls after a day's treatment were not going to be an option. People were kept updated by text and it worked well too. This became the norm then for every eventuality throughout Hubby's illness, a group text to keep people in the loop and up to speed with his progress. A return text usually thanked us for letting them know, wishing us all the best and offering any help we may need. Perfect system.

Lara's Story

Telling everyone about the diagnosis was difficult and, I think, has to be done in a way that best suits the person who has the disease which can vary significantly. There are those who want no-one to know, those who want everyone to know and those who only want immediate family and the people at work who have to be told to know. Nick decided that everyone in the family, friends and work should all be told. First our sons had to be told. That was one of the hardest moments from the whole five years. We sat at the kitchen table and just told them what we knew. Their dad had cancer, it was incurable but his oncologist said that he was fit and young and they were going to treat the disease aggressively. Nick was going to accept all the treatment that could be thrown at him. They had questions which we answered, there were tears and hugs and Nick, as was his way, cracked a joke or two. I'm sure both boys went off to their computers and started googling like mad as over the next few days there were more questions and they understood more about the situation. They were sad, angry about the delayed diagnosis but supportive and relieved a treatment plan was in place.

Telling Nick's family was also hard. His parents didn't seem to register what we were telling them, how ill he was or that his cancer was stage 4. There were no questions just "you'll be fine, you're young and strong" type comments. His brothers were very negative; one sat and told us how his boss had died in a short space of time from bowel cancer and his other brother, when we explained that his age and health were on his side and he could have quite some time left with us, disagreed and just pointed out that once the cancer had spread as extensively as Nick's had there was no chance of a positive treatment outcome, he was dying and that was that.

My family got on board with the let's give treatment a go approach. They were visibly upset but encouraging and offered to help us in any way they could. We wouldn't have managed nearly as well without them over those 5 years.

We chose not to tell friends face to face but instead to write to them. There were two reasons for this; firstly it is draining and upsetting passing on the news time after time and secondly it gave people a chance for the news to sink in before they responded. Most people, I think, were grateful for this approach. We wrote different emails to different groups of friends. To our closest friends we were detailed and totally honest about how things were, to friends with children who were friends of the boys we asked them to tell their children so they would understand if the boys were not themselves and we knew they would look out for them. To other friends we wrote another letter and to work colleagues another.

As treatment started and time passed we updated people of Nick's progress or changes in the same way. It was an approach that worked for us. Even though his cancer was incurable there was positive news to share. Every scan the news was any one of three things; there were more and/or larger tumours which was never good, there was no change which was good or there were fewer/smaller tumours showing which was great. With an incurable diagnosis you take the positives where you can find them.

We weren't contacting people on a weekly or even monthly basis. What we did was update them when there was a big change in Nick's situation, before he was having surgery so they were aware he would be in hospital and after scans.

Some people would write asking how Nick was and so I replied. When I got no response to that reply I found it quite hard. Why ask if you do nothing with the information. Why ask if you are going to offer no support, even a few lines of written support, to the family. I have to admit as time went on there were some people who I stopped updating.

Work

As a carer you may or may not be working, you may or may not have a choice to continue to work or to stop, bills still keep coming in, the cost of living doesn't vanish and indeed may well go up with increased travel bills and heating bills. If your loved one was working at some stage that may stop. Whatever your situation, finances could effected.

But work isn't necessarily all about finances. It may be that having the structure and normality of work with the interaction with your colleagues can be helpful, good for you. Equally you could have a stressful job, a job with lots of responsibility, a job you loathe. Your employer may be supportive, some may not. Carers have a right to request flexible working and a right to time off for dependants in an emergency (which may or may not be paid). Knowing your rights can be useful.

There is no right or wrong to what you decide to do and whatever decisions you make, within the restrictions of your individual situation, hopefully colleagues, family and friends will be supportive.

Suzanna

The situation with Mark's employers was very awkward. No diagnosis equalled vague sick notes which left them understandably curious about his prolonged absence. As the weeks rolled round it became standard procedure for them to send for him to be interviewed, regarding his absence. Hubby explained that he was undergoing tests at the time.

By the time of his second work review, Hubby looked dreadful. On spotting him, the union rep came across and offered to attend the review with him. The rep then told Mark's bosses that you only had to look at him to see he was a very sick man, who should be left in peace until the results were back.

Once we had a firm diagnosis of terminal cancer, they backed right off and the reviews stopped. They continued to pay him a full wage until he died. In fact they became a lot more sensitive and supportive, once they realised Hubby would never return to work again.

I have to say my employers were very understanding indeed, right from the onset .They always asked how Mark was. I was working when he first became ill and I found it hard not to be permanently worried and distracted by his undiagnosed illness. I knew he was desperately ill, but not what with and hoped with all my heart that it wasn't cancer. I was always allowed time off to attend Hubby's investigations and follow up appointments.

I really didn't wish to discuss Mark's illness at work, especially when his health declined even further. It started to make me feel very upset when colleague's asked me how he was. I worked in a Secondary School, I needed to be cool, calm and collected at all times. I couldn't afford to lose my composure in front of the students.

I had devised three really basic answers to people's enquiries of Mark's health. Short and to the point: same as - bit better - bit worse. As far as I was concerned at the time, they answered the question, but didn't dwell on the subject long enough to make me upset and distressed, thinking about my poor husband.

If it came across as rude, it certainly wasn't meant to be. It was just another coping strategy I had invented to get me by. Occasionally I opened up to close colleagues about my fears, but not very often and not in any depth.

When Hubby was finally diagnosed with Lung cancer, we were reeling with shock. I rang into School and confided in my Boss. I requested she informed staff and asked them not to question me, as I was barely holding myself together at home, without discussing it at work too.

Most people honoured my wishes, but a few felt the need to comfort me or offer support. A few hugged me silently, but that was fine by me. When Mark needed me at home to care for him I took voluntary redundancy which, by sheer coincidence, was on offer at the time. This gave me the opportunity to be by Mark's side constantly. It was as if it was meant to be, right time, right place for once.

I kept in touch with my colleagues though, their support and company became invaluable. A while after Hubby's death, I went back to work part time, doing exam invigilation and helping out when and where I could. It stopped me from being so sad, bored and lonely. It also got me out of the house, distracting me from my loss and giving me less time to dwell on my situation. I have some lovely friends there that I am happy to spend time with and it feels as if I am back where I belong.

Lara's Story

Work had always been hugely important to Nick, something he loved, and when he was diagnosed he continued to work, mainly from home, for as long as he could. He worked throughout his first course of chemotherapy, took a brief break for major surgery, and then went back to work and worked through his first course of radiotherapy. It wasn't easy and took its toll but it was what he wanted to do. When he was no longer able to work we were fortunate that he had critical illness insurance and he continued to be paid a percentage of his salary.

The company he worked for were fantastic, I can't fault the way that the Human Resources team behaved. They were understanding, flexible and professional, we couldn't have asked for more. Unfortunately, from what I have read and been told, it seems not every company is as supportive to either a person with cancer or to a carer.

I, on the other hand, was working for a local charity and, because his illness was so advanced, left as soon as I could. Before his diagnosis Nick had been away from Monday to Friday for work and spent some weekends travelling, so for some years we hadn't spent much time together as a family. There were most weekends and holidays but that was all. I accepted this lifestyle because I knew how important work was to Nick and I told myself that when he retired we would have all the time we wanted together. Well, that time wasn't going to happen and so I wanted to spend all the time I could with my dear man and to be there whenever he needed me. We were in a fortunate position that Nick was still being paid part of his salary which we could live on.

We had no idea that we would get five years together and I was grateful for every day but there were days that I wished for some normality, something that made me more than "the carer" and gave me a life outside cancer.

After he died the isolation I felt, and still feel, I think was made worse by not having a job to return to or the confidence to go and find one. Caring for a prolonged period can strip you of so much you end up having to take time to remember who you were before you were forced into that role.

After a couple of years of Nick's illness I started to work as a volunteer for a cancer charity, a role I could carry out from home when Nick was resting or sleeping. It let me use my experience to help others in a similar situation but it didn't let me escape cancer or my role as a carer. I also completed an Open University introductory course to give me something to do, again while Nick slept or rested. It did me good although meeting deadlines sometimes put me under unneeded pressure. I have recently stopped the charity work and am beginning to look for a new path to travel, something completely different, but first there is this book to finish.

The Treatment Plan

Suzanna

While you're already dealing with letting family, friends and work know, the wait for a treatment plan has started. It can vary and, if lengthy, it leaves you worrying that the cancer could be spreading even more widely. In Mark's case the wait was unavoidable, as he was now an inpatient with pulmonary embolisms and would need time to recover before any treatment was even considered.

The treatment plan is usually decided by a Multi-Disciplinary Team (MDT). This will consist of a group of medical professionals with expertise in the relevant type of cancer. Together they will hold a meeting, look at the scans and general health status, then debate and decide the best plan of action possible for the individual case. I guess for Mark there would have been varying opinions to what the best plan would be.

The MDT would have taken into consideration the stage and size of the cancer and how they thought Mark would cope with any treatment available. The specialist discussed each option with us and it was then up to Mark to consider the offers, accepting or declining them. He would have been free to choose no treatment at all, if that was his wish.

When the decision was made to accept treatment, Mark was given a consent form to sign and an information sheet on the combination of chemo drugs to be used. He also received a list of possible side effects, plus what to do in the case of post chemo complications.

We found it good to have each other at this important decision making appointment. We listened very carefully, I took notes and gave Mark moral support. Two heads are always better than one, it's easy to miss important pieces of information or forget bits under pressure, as the whole situation is very stressful.

Our first meeting with the oncologist was at Mark's bedside. As he was still an inpatient at the time, he kindly visited him on the ward. I can remember thinking how incredibly young he looked, or were we just getting older?

His initial offer of treatment was a small dose of chemo, lasting approximately 3 hours. As Mark was so ill, the oncologist felt this low key treatment would be the most he could cope with at the time. Mark agreed and accepted his offer, so he arranged an outpatient appointment to see him again.

We next saw the oncologist in clinic. He greeted us warmly and said he had had a change of heart. Taking into consideration that Mark was still relatively young and with all he had been through, yet bounced back from (his Macmillan Nurse called him Superman), he was now prepared to offer him a full course of treatment.

This would consist of 4 cycles of full day chemo with a combination of drugs. We were told this combination produced the best results for his cancer type. He felt as Hubby was so strong, he would cope with it after all. Although he was going at it very much 'gung ho' style, he felt it would pay dividends in the long run.

Mark would have 2 cycles, then a scan, 2 more cycles, then another scan. This would be followed by maintenance chemo, to hopefully keep any shrinkage at bay. We were given the relevant paperwork, an appointment for a chemo talk, for bloods to be taken and also for a visit to the chemo ward to have a look round and familiarise ourselves with the surroundings and set up of the ward.

Mark maintained he would always accept any treatment offered, he was so desperate to shrink his tumours. I, on the other hand, felt a little more cautious. I was really worried about how much the chemo would take its toll on his already fragile state of health and fully aware of the risks and side effects that could possibly trip us up, or even be fatal along the way, especially given hubby's angina. But, ultimately it was Mark's decision, his body, his choice to make. I would readily accept his decision and be there, by his side, waiting to nurse him through whatever event occurred during treatment. It would be tough for him to endure and very hard for me to watch him go through it all, but together we would cope. I just needed to stay focused and in control at all times, a big ask. I was having to learn fast to swallow down my anxieties and overwhelming sadness. Rightly or wrongly, this was my coping mechanism.

The day of the appointment arrived and initially we were taken into a little office for a pre chemo chat with a specialist nurse, she told us all we needed to know and answered our questions. She was patient and kind and made time for us, making sure we understood everything that was about to happen to Mark. Then they took blood, or tried to as his poor veins wouldn't give it easily, they had to send for a nurse who was known to be able to get blood from difficult veins, but even she had a struggle, eventually she managed to get some from the side of his thumb, but this was very painful for Mark and knocked him about, he was oxygen dependant at the time so not at all well.

Once that was done we were given a guided tour of the chemo ward. It was busy, every comfy seat taken by a patient, hooked up to treatment. Some had a companion with them, some sat alone, snoozing, reading, chatting or even knitting. The Nurses' Station was situated in the centre of the room, giving them a perfect view of all the patients surrounding them. Mark was then weighed and measured. A few patients smiled and waved at us, guessing it was our first visit to the unit and how nervous we must be.

We were then ushered back to the office, where we were given an appointment for Mark's first cycle of chemo and full day at the unit. Everything was now set in place for treatment, we just had to be prepared physically and emotionally for it. It would be a long day, but we were ready.

Lara

Whoever coined the phrase "patience is a virtue" had never had to spend time waiting for a treatment plan to be drawn up when all you want is for that treatment to start.

All employees at Nick's company were covered by private health insurance. A lot of his treatment was carried out privately, some was carried out by the NHS, both were exemplary. I am sure this meant that he had options that some people don't have in terms of treatment, he was very fortunate, but the impact of treatment on all of the family was still horribly tough.

As he had used his insurance to get the second colonoscopy that lead to his diagnosis he was referred to an oncologist privately. Before a plan could be made every test under the sun, and then a few more, had to be carried out. Nick had his heart and kidney function tested, several scans, blood tests and other tests too. Because they were considering throwing the full arsenal at him in terms of treatment they needed to be sure he was fit enough to withstand it.

The wait was hard. I had visions of the cancer developing more and spreading further while we waited, although there wasn't much further it could spread.

There was no MDT meeting to discuss Nick's case. Instead there was the sending of letters and scans between oncologist, radiologist and various surgeons which seemed to take forever. But, eventually, there was a plan.

None of the cancer was operable and it was too wide spread for radiotherapy so chemotherapy it was. While Nick was desperate to get started I was both dreading it and wanting to get a move on at the same time. I had seen how ill her treatment had made a very good friend of mine and was worried and scared about how Nick would respond. The word chemo provoked thoughts of vomiting and nausea, hair loss and skin problems, nose bleeds and so much more. My poor dear Nick, I hated the thought of what he was about to go through.

It was going to be initially 6 months of chemotherapy with a scan after 3 months, on a fortnightly cycle with one day on the chemo ward and then two days at home with a chemo pump attached before returning to hospital to have it removed. As long as there was a positive response to the treatment after 6 months they would rescan and review what next.

So that was that. We had a tour of the chemo ward and were talked through everything by one of the nurses. Looking around I realised that before long it would be Nick in one of those chairs attached to drips. One last thing had to happen before the chemo started, Nick had to have a portacath fitted under his skin with a tube connecting the port directly into a vein for them to use for the treatment.

Chemotherapy

Suzanna

Mark was now ready to start chemotherapy. I was both in awe, and afraid in equal measures, of the treatment he'd receive. Chemotherapy is a massive intrusive attack on the body, it needs to be. It seeks out cancerous cells and attempts to stop them reproducing or eradicate them. But it also attacks other healthy, cells at the same time. It can wipe out your immune system, leaving you weak, run down and vulnerable to infection. I was dreading the after effects, but here we were waiting for his first session to commence.

His first session was to start at 8.30 am sharp, but we had to book hospital transport there and back, as Mark was now oxygen dependent and needed to be plugged into the ambulance supply to travel. Unfortunately they don't start pickups until 8.30 and then they collect a few patients at a time, meaning we were late before we even started out. I rang the ward to say we were running late, but they said don't worry, just get there as quickly as possible. We were more than an hour late for the session, meaning we were there till 9pm, an incredibly long day for Mark's first session.

Bag after bag of liquids were pumped into him intravenously, some just fluids, some toxic chemo drugs. I sat with him and together we watched the drip, drip, drip of the fluid in the bags enter his body. We hoped with all our hearts that this treatment would shrink his tumours and give him some more precious time. One of our Macmillan nurses popped in to see how he was coping and sat chatting to us for a while **which helped** us to settle into the treatment room more comfortably, calmed both of our nerves and answered some of our outstanding questions.

Mark was given a vitamin B injection, iron tablets, anti-sickness drugs and steroids, all to try to prevent some of the nasty side effects caused by chemo. At lunch time he was offered some freshly made veg soup which smelt lovely, I could have eaten some myself. With some coaxing, he managed to eat it to help keep his strength up. Eventually, he'd had every bag and every tablet needed and we could go home. We were taken home by ambulance and settled down quietly for the night after a few phone calls **from friends and family,** enquiring about Mark's day.

The following morning he woke up with a dreadful rash all over his face, neck and chest. He was very confused and agitated, he grabbed our tub of biro pens and started to strip them down, swopping the insides around. He was also trying to pick up invisible items, like someone delirious. He was incredibly breathless, even with oxygen. I felt **way** out of my depth, but luckily for us the District Nurses were visiting at the time and so I didn't have long to wait for advice or reassurance .

When the Nurse was present Mark had an angina attack, I gave him his GTN spray and the nurse rang the ward with his list of symptoms. They told her to monitor him carefully and if he became worse, they would admit him. Luckily all the symptoms calmed down as the day progressed. By the next day Mark couldn't remember any of it and I heaved a sigh of relief. He was left with a very sore mouth and was unable to eat, but a few days later his breathing had improved remarkably and he was without the dreadful continual headache for the first time in several months. We were absolutely delighted and felt the chemo must be working, maybe shrinking the tumours and taking the pressure off surrounding nerves.

By Mark's second chemo session, there was already a big change in his health, he was barely using any oxygen at all and remained headache free. To us this was like winning the lottery and the chemo nurses were both amazed and delighted when he arrived for his next chemo session. Our son dropped us in this time, as no oxygen equalled no ambulance and happily we were on time. When we arrived there was another man there, undergoing exactly the same treatment, he too had lung cancer. I got chatting to his wife and, in time, we became firm friends while our two men started to talk to each other. Another long day of treatment as before, but at least we had our new friends to pass the day with this time. It's amazing how a conversation and a bit of light-hearted banter and company can lighten the load of a heavy day. The time seemed to pass faster in company.

At home the next day we had a repeat of the rash, although we weren't so startled by it this time. But Mark was even more agitated and confused than last time. I had to sit up all night with him, as he found it impossible to sit down or relax in any way, it took me back to the days when our boys were ill and needed me as children. Mark was messing with everything, like a toddler would. He grabbed his liquid morphine bottle, unscrewed the lid and proceeded to try and drink the contents, like a bottle of pop. Thank goodness I was awake and on top of his antics, or heaven knows what could have happened that night! After that I kept the morphine hidden away.

The following morning when the District Nurses arrived, I was totally exhausted. Mark later said they hadn't been for two days, as again, he could remember nothing of the post chemo days. But I could, and it was very hard going. He had another angina attack which was far more severe than the last one, lasting longer, but it eventually subsided with his GTN spray and rest. This time round Mark lost some hair and also pigmentation, in fact his remaining hair seemed to go white overnight. His former brown locks gone, he now sported hair that resembled white candy floss.

A few days later he developed a chest infection. The District Nurse called our GP out and he was given antibiotics. His mouth became incredibly sore again, with both ulcers and thrush, he was not able to eat at all so he was prescribed build up drinks in a fruity flavour. He sipped at those and luckily he liked them.

Once everything settled back down, his breathing was much improved and he actually felt better than he had in a long time. We felt that all the side effects had been worthwhile as now he could potter around the house and was, incredibly, totally oxygen free. This was half way through chemo, as he could only have four cycles at full strength.

The third chemo was yet another long day session, but we sat with our new friends again, as our husbands' chemo sessions coincided with each other. We even managed a few laughs during the day, as our Hubbies competed to get their next bag of chemo going, therefore complete their treatment day first. It broke the tension and I even managed to go for my counselling session during the day, as we seemed to be slipping into some sort of routine, if you can call it that. I still meet my friend for a coffee and an update regularly. Her Husband continued to battle on with this awful disease for another two years, when sadly he lost his fight too.

After this third cycle Mark became very anaemic, needing a blood transfusion in the Day Case Unit to pick him back up. Post chemo he had yet another angina attack, repeated loss of memory and his sore mouth became much worse this time, I could have cried for him. He shed his skin, like a snake, flakes of skin were all through the house. It was all over his clothes, on the floor, furniture, just everywhere so I was continually vacuuming.

His ankles were dreadfully swollen by now and I was moisturising his whole body, it was so dry. Understandably Mark became depressed and incredibly tired. Before the fourth and final chemo cycle there was a gap, to give his poor body a chance to recover from the gruelling treatment and for his blood count to pick back up.

His last full day on the chemo unit was followed by yet another nasty angina attack, which were becoming way too frequent. Yet another chest infection, needing the GP out again. He was checked over, given even stronger antibiotics, plus new angina tablets to try to reduce the frequency of attacks, also a new mouthwash for his incredibly sore mouth. My heart went out to him, he was prepared to suffer any treatment and any side effects, to prolong his life. He was so brave, he never gave up and I was really proud of him.

After this final cycle Mark developed a very swollen abdomen and ended up spending a day in the EAU **(Emergency Assessment** Unit) so he could be seen by a doctor. They put him on water tablets, yet another symptom and yet more medication to add to his ever growing list.

Looking back it sounds horrendous but, in between cycles, he did have really good days amidst the bad ones. As treatment progressed you could almost predict which days would be good and which would be bad. Therefore we could plan days out, special occasions, even a mini break away on his 'good week', which sadly was followed by two bad ones.

Hubby's scan, post chemo, was now due as all four full chemo cycles had been completed. He would have his scan, then an appointment with his oncologist to discuss ongoing treatment plus the results of the scan. He was due to have maintenance chemo next, to keep any shrinkage at bay, but that would depend widely on his scan results plus the state of his health. He had now developed a blood sugar problem plus the start of a niggly headache had returned, which was very concerning. But we decided not to start panicking, rather wait for the scan and its results. We would see the oncologist and wait on what he had to say about the way forward from here on in.

Lara

Our first trip to the chemo suite at the hospital happened directly after the oncology appointment outlining the treatment that was planned for Nick. We talked to one of the nurses there about what chemo would involve, looked around, and Nick had blood taken and was weighed, something that happened before each treatment.

There were several people sitting in comfy chairs with drips feeding various poisonous cocktails into their arm or their chest. Some were on iPads or computers, some sleeping, others talking quietly to a companion or reading a book, most snuggled under blankets. The atmosphere was surprisingly calm and the nurses were friendly and attentive. Those nurses who we saw over the next 5 years were so good at their job. I saw them spring into action on a few occasions to help a patient who was having a panic attack, or an allergic reaction, or just feeling overwhelmed. They were always busy, always professional, and so kind.

The first type of treatment Nick had involved a day on the chemo suite, having various chemical concoctions pumped into his body and then him coming home with a bottle that was attached via the portacath for the next 48 hours slowly feeding more chemicals into his blood stream. Then returning to the unit to have the empty bottle removed. I remember feeling very anxious that first day.

How would he react to the drugs? Would he feel nauseous? Would he be able to sleep with the steroids he'd been given to take for 3 or 4 days? What side effects would he get? However nice the staff were, and however much they explained things, everything had just become very real. Seeing my gentle man sitting there hooked up to bag after bag of drugs was the first time he looked like a person with cancer. While he was joking with the staff or asking questions I was sitting there with a smile on my face joining in, but inside feeling a rising sense of panic. I remember hoping that my voice sounded normal and calm, not showing the turmoil within.

Over the next five years Nick had over 50 cycles of chemo of different types. Although there were times that his bloods weren't good enough, or he was ill and the chemo was delayed, it always went ahead eventually. Nick was assured that the chemotherapy stayed in the blood for many weeks and so we didn't worry that the odd delay would impact the effectiveness of treatment. His portacath needed replacing once when the catheter ruptured (luckily while being flushed with saline rather than feeding a toxic chemotherapy drugs which might have done considerable damage) but other than that chemo happened. Over and over again.

Nick tried to think of chemo in a positive way, although it was doing damage to his body it was also doing damage to the cancer. He visualised what was happening inside his body as a game of pac-man, with the pac chemo-man chasing and eating the pac cancer-dots.

After the first session he preferred it if I didn't stay with him. Although hard, I had to respect that so I would take him in the morning with something to eat and his chemo record book, stay while the blood tests were carried out, and make sure he had everything he needed. I'd then leave, alone if his bloods were good, with him if they weren't. In the early months he worked on his laptop, slept and chatted with other cancer patients and the staff. As time went on he slept more, read little and stopped working but he did have his iPod with recorded radio programmes and news reports that he listened to. Nick was never without a radio, radio 4 or the BBC World Service were always playing somewhere in the house and podcasts took their place on hospital days.

Once, when getting up from his desk at home the tube from the chemo bottle got caught around the chair arm and the pin fixing it to the portacath ripped. What was in the tube spilt over him and me as we tried to see what had happened but we soon managed to close the pump off so no more could spill and phoned the chemo ward. We were told, very calmly, to come to the hospital immediately so set off in the car to be greeted by a chemo nurse dressed in overalls and gloves who took us a back route into a small room to remove the bottle and check the port. We hadn't thought about the toxicity of the chemicals in the bottle and that most of them can cause significant damage to the skin but that was why the nurse was gowned and gloved. On realising Nick had the same clothes on, he had to remove them and put on a hospital gown. The clothes were sent for incineration I think, I just needed my hands and arms washed off thoroughly. Eventually, after a new bottle had been reattached to the portacath, and after being told how to manage a spillage if it were to happen again, we were sent home with a spill hazard clean up kit. We did get some strange looks as Nick walked through the hospital out to the car in a hospital gown, furry slipper boots and my bright red coat, with me carrying a large yellow bucket with hazard warning symbols on it.

Over time and different types of chemotherapy he suffered many side effects including nausea, several skin conditions, an increased number of allergies, hair loss (partial not complete), weak nails that split and tore easily, severe peripheral neuropathy, exhaustion, sensitivity to cold, thrush, nose bleeds, loss of/ changing taste, nasal drip, upset stomach, altered vision, and headaches. He rarely vomited unlike my friend who, while on oral chemo, would regularly redecorate the downstairs toilet with a bout of projectile vomiting. Some of the more serious side effects were pulmonary embolisms and excruciating ulceration of the mouth and throat.

Most of these side effects were well controlled or improved with other medications. The ulceration was a different matter, totally horrific and made my stomach churn to see what he was putting up with. One very strange side effect caused by one type of chemotherapy was that his eyelashes grew, thick and so long I had to trim them with nail scissors. When a friend visited one day he took one look at Nick, did a double take at his lashes, flushed cheeks and bright red lips from the chemo and declared "Bloody hell Nick, you look like an aged panto dame who's forgotten her wig". Trust a friend to tell it as it is!

We learnt quickly not to let Nick suffer in silence. If side effects are becoming unbearable tell the oncology department, there are things that can be done. There are meds that help alleviate the nausea and sickness, some lotions are better for the skin than others, there are shampoos that can be recommended for a sensitive scalp, ways of treating the thrush, an upset stomach and ways to deal with nose bleeds, tablets or injections to prevent a recurrence of PEs. Even mouth washes for the ulceration but that needs to be caught early or it can take several painful weeks to sort out. Some weeks we left the hospital with two carrier bags full of prescription items. A small reduction in the dose of medication can make a big difference to side effects. I think Nick had his dose reduced on two courses of chemotherapy. It wasn't something he wanted to do but it turned out to be the best decision in terms of improving quality of life.

Things we learnt:

- Don't go empty handed for a day in the chemo ward. Think about taking a book, a paper, and if Wi-Fi is available a tablet or laptop.
- Many units offer lunch but it may not be something your loved one can face. You could take an alternative and remember something for yourself.
- A warm jumper can come in handy (blankets may be available).
- If going home with a chemo bottle attached make sure you have a spill pack and know what to do if the

line comes out or gets pulled out and the chemicals get on the skin.
- Always know what side effects to look out for, who to contact and when. Don't be afraid to ring the chemo unit for advice or help if you feel you need it.
- Have a thermometer at home. A below normal temperature needs watching as well as a raised one.
- If the treatment causes nose bleeds a cold compress on the forehead works much better than pinching the bridge of the nose.
- Don't do big shops, you could find what your loved one will try to eat can change on an almost a daily basis.
- Regular use of a good cream can really help skin problems such as dried and cracked skin. Caring for the skin is very important.
- Always carry the chemo book when you go out and any warning cards you may be given (for example a steroid use card).
- Talk about whether your loved one wants company at chemo or would prefer to be alone. It is a personal choice.
- A good pair of really warm slippers and shoes or boots can be useful for peripheral neuropathy and gloves if going outside.

Surgery

Lara

His first course of chemo was so successful Nick was then offered surgery to remove the primary tumour. Nick had a significant amount of surgery during his 5 years of treatment, which ranged from relatively straightforward surgery to some very major surgery indeed. His response to chemo was so good that the surgery became an option which he readily accepted.

The more straightforward operations included fitting or replacing his portacath and fitting a stent to help keep his airway open. He underwent major bowel surgery to remove the primary tumour once the chemo had shrunk it so much that surgery became possible, two liver resections, and three lung operations during which he lost over 50% of his lungs. In his mind, surgery was the most effective way of getting rid of cancer and the initial pain and then the recovery period seemed a price worth paying for this.

The first major operation was to remove the primary colorectal tumour. It would be major surgery, could leave him with a colostomy or ileostomy and may mean the removal of his seminal vesicles, we were also told he might suffer urinary incontinence and impotence after the operation.

Nick often said that as a person with incurable cancer there were no good choices, only choices. His choice here was possibly extending the time he had to live while facing life changing outcomes from the surgery or facing the probability of living less long without these particular outcomes but the likelihood of other affects as the tumour grew. He chose the surgery.

The evening before the operation he was admitted to hospital. I spent some hours with him trying to hide my nerves before going home to a sleepless night. Nick never wanted me to be at the hospital during surgery. He said there was no point, I would just be sitting around on hard chairs in sterile corridors or a waiting room feeling tense and stressing when I could be at home in familiar surroundings, trying to occupy myself. I understood his logic but being at home wasn't much easier, especially the first time. I couldn't relax but neither could I focus on anything. I would start one thing and then, thinking about what my husband was going through, forget what that thing was and start another in an attempt to distract myself. If anyone phoned I became irritated, I needed the phones free in case the hospital wanted to contact me and told the callers this as calmly as I could manage. The surgery was scheduled to take between 7 and 8 hours. In the event it took over 9. I called and was told he was still in surgery, still in surgery, then in recovery.

Eventually I was told Nick would spend the night on the recovery ward and move to the High Dependency Unit in the morning. The surgery had been "complicated but successful" and I could visit him once he was in HDU. Complicated. What did that mean? Another restless night before I could go and find out.

Early the next morning I was back on the phone, the night had been uneventful and Nick was moving to the HDU. Uneventful was good, I could stop holding my breath and head off to be with him.

Poor Nick was draped with wires, tubes, drains and drips. He was obviously in some pain and still a little muddled from a sleepless night and the pain meds. My heart wept to see him that way. He was in hospital for over 2 weeks as an infection took hold after the first week and he nearly ended up in HDU again. It was a scary time and each day as I headed up to the hospital I had to steel myself. Days were spent sitting by his bed, fetching and carrying, helping him move around, distracting him with news from home and reading emails from friends. We became quite good at tackling newspaper crosswords and puzzles together and dreaming up our hospital escape plans when being there just got too much for him. Other visitors were limited, Nick was tired and in pain and didn't want people to see him that way. The boys went to see him but found it quite distressing so often would just email, text or phone to chat. Slowly he became stronger and then at last was let home.

Nick had arrived at hospital outwardly fit having coped well with the months of chemo that proceeded surgery. He left weak, in pain, pooing and peeing into bags and impotent. But the tumour had been removed and, with 6 weeks of radiotherapy, part of the belts and braces approach, it never returned. He got stronger, the pain reduced, and the catheter was removed after about 6 weeks when the inflammation had subsided and he could pee again. The ileostomy, although intended to be temporary became permanent.

In hindsight it may have been better for him to have had a colostomy, easier to manage and allowing him to absorb more of the nutrients in his food. The impotence was also permanent and no treatment, pills, or gadgets could resolve that. Nick had a philosophy in life that worrying or fretting about things you can't influence is a waste of energy that could be used more positively on other matters. So, he pooed into a bag which was stuck on his stomach with glue. Well, he just had to focus on his diet to make sure he got the best nutrition he could. The physical side of our relationship had changed for ever, so we just had to focus on the other parts. I wish I could have dealt with things as he did but he was Mr Head and I was Mrs Heart and although I had no problem with the ileostomy I found the loss of intimacy hard to accept for quite some time.

But he was alive and the tumour had gone so, incredibly, he accepted the outcome and prepared to move on to tackling the secondary tumours in his liver and lungs. I wasn't like Nick and couldn't rationalise things away as easily as he seemed to but I tried. After a couple of months though he recovered and was feeling better than he had in a long while and at that stage we believe the ileostomy bag was a temporary measure. He was pleased that he'd had the operation and I was relieved he had recovered so well.

And so was the pattern of treatment; chemo, surgery, radiotherapy, chemo, surgery, surgery, radiotherapy, chemo, surgery…. an endless and relentless cycle that not many people would have put themselves through or endured so calmly and positively.

For some reason the lung surgery scared me more than any other. I didn't even know that it was possible to operate on a person's lungs before Nick became ill. The first operation he recovered from remarkably quickly but then his lung capacity had been excellent. They had him on an exercise bike within days, even before the drains were removed. The second was a little tougher but he was still peddling on a bike next to his bed very quickly.

Nick never said that he wished he hadn't had so much surgery. The only treatment he regretted was his final course of chemotherapy where the side effects were cruel and unbearable in the extreme. What would have happened without the surgery? Who knows. Every operation was tough and really hard for me and the boys as well as him. But he did recover well and none were as harsh in terms of side effects as that first big operation.

Things we learnt

- Surgery can be unpredictable, until the surgeon gets inside they aren't always sure exactly what they will find.
- If you are aware of the possible effects of the surgery you will feel better prepared, some aren't obvious and so it is worth doing your reading and asking questions prior to surgery. Knowing the longer term implications of the surgery can help you make an informed decision.
- Not all of the effects are permanent, some unfortunately could be.
- Your loved one may seem more ill directly after surgery and for the recovery period than they did before going into hospital.
- The external scar needs care while healing. Follow care instructions and seek advice if the scar looks inflamed or weepy.
- Internal scar tissue can cause tissue and organs to adhere together causing a number of problems such as discomfort, pain, and obstruction (for example of the bowel). This can happen at any time after surgery so be aware of the signs.

Radiotherapy

Lara

Mark didn't have radiotherapy but Nick did.

After surgery to remove the primary tumour in Nick's colon the surgeon recommended that it was followed with 6 weeks of radiotherapy to "mop up" any stray cells. As the tumour had been large and invasive he wanted a belts and braces approach and Nick was happy with this.

The first appointment at the hospital was for all the measurements to be taken and to mark Nick with little permanent tattoo dots that they would use to line him up with the machine each day. It was a little more complicated because he couldn't lie on his stomach as they would have preferred. The stoma didn't allow that, but they found a way around the problem so that he could lie on his back for the treatment. Joking with the boys about his tattoos he was ready as always to crack on. For some radiotherapy, depending on the area targeted, the preparation can differ. Radiotherapy to the head and neck for example involves a mask being made. I imagine, for some people, wearing a mask must add to any stress they are already feeling.

For Nick, the treatment sessions themselves were fine, half an hour to hospital, a short wait, 15 minutes in the treatment room and half an hour home. We were lucky to be relatively near the hospital.

Side effects from radiotherapy are cumulative, building up in number and strength during the course of the treatment and for a few weeks afterwards. They only start to subside two to three weeks after treatment has finished. The first effect for Nick was fatigue. He was exhausted and this got worse as the treatments added up. The next was sore skin but we dealt with that by applying oodles of an appropriate moisturiser both before and after treatment and again every evening. This was really important to avoid sore cracked skin. He also had some bloating and stomach cramps and some diarrhoea. Diarrhoea can be dangerous with an ileostomy as a person can become dehydrated incredibly quickly so Nick took meds to help with this. By the end of the 6 weeks he had had enough, 2 weeks after this he was totally fed up with the exhaustion, then things began to improve. The cancer never returned to his bowel so all in all he felt the treatment was worthwhile.

The second course of radiotherapy was to his upper chest area and the side effects were far more severe. By the end of the course he was struggling to both eat and talk. Three weeks later he was even worse and had no voice at all. I tried to put lots of key sentences, words and phrases on a free voice simulator on the iPad for him to use, we had fun with this for a few days but then he reverted to writing messages to me or using hand signals. I got used to asking questions that only required a nod or shake of the head, a thumbs up or down, as an answer. He slept a lot due to the exhaustion, was weak and felt generally rotten. Sleep gave some escape. As things gradually improved so did his sense of humour and my sanity. He was able to eat again and regained some strength. Although his appetite and interest in food never seemed to fully recover I don't think this was solely down to the radiotherapy.

Although most of the side effects subsided there was some permanent damage. His voice never fully recovered, remained weak and he often only talked in a whisper. I missed his voice. He did too. His skin in the areas targeted remained dark in colour, was much more delicate and the body hair never grew back.

It is hard going for both the carer and the person having any treatment. The daily trips to hospital with someone who may be feeling very ill already, the waiting around, the extra care needed at home, the "what might they be able to eat?", and the loneliness while they sleep off the effects of the treatment can be tough for the carer. I kept telling myself that it was worth it. After surgery, we were told, radiotherapy was the second most effective treatment against cancer. In his case it was worthwhile and that is what we kept reminding ourselves. And we were lucky to live in the city and to be able to drive to the hospital, also that Nick was still independently mobile. I accompanied my friend on a couple of occasions to a session and, with the long drive in from the countryside and the waiting around, it was a far more tiring experience. By the time we got home that was the day done.

Radiotherapy doesn't always last as many weeks. It can be a week or two or even a single session if it is for pain relief purposes for example in the case of bone cancer. I think the longest course is 5 days a week for 6 weeks, at least I haven't heard of anyone having longer than this.

Family and friends saw radiotherapy as an easy treatment, far easier than chemotherapy and surgery. They aren't aware of the side effects or the lasting damage it can cause especially if the course lasts any length of time. I wasn't aware of the impact it could have until Nick experienced it. Like all the cancer treatment he had there was a big payoff for the benefit, but there was a benefit.

Things we learnt:

- The person undergoing treatment could think about wearing clothes that are easy to remove if it is going to be necessary to undress. Most radiotherapy departments work to a very tight timescale, to maximise the number of appointments they can fit in, and easily slipping something on or off can reduce the stress.
- Ask about skin care and what creams are best to use. This may be available on prescription.
- You should have the possible side effects of treatment explained to you. If not, ask. It is better to be prepared. As usual there are likely to be medications available to help reduce the impact of these so don't suffer in silence.
- Side effects are cumulative and at their worse two to three weeks after the treatment has finished before gradually subsiding. Bear this in mind if making plans.

Infection

Lara

Infections can occur at any time, not just during treatment periods but there were times when Nick seemed to be more susceptible. Post operation, during a course of chemo and, as time went on, he suffered from an increasing number.

His first big infection was after he had undergone bowel surgery to remove the primary tumour. The operation was long but successful and Nick was out of the High Dependency Unit and back on the ward. After a couple of days he started being violently sick, managing to achieve a techni-colour redecoration of his bed, and a poor nurse, in a matter of moments. He got worse, had a high fever and was being closely monitored by the HDU doctors in case they needed to move him back to their unit. He became delirious, looked seriously unwell and I was very concerned and upset.

My parents dropped everything and came to stay and hold the fort at home so I could spend more time at the hospital which was a huge relief as I hated leaving him when he was so ill. The doctors and nurses were excellent and looked after him well. All I could do was fetch and carry, talk to Nick, hold his hand, and make sure he was as comfortable as possible.

Some of the hardest times were when Nick was at home and didn't seem well. It felt like a huge responsibility to make the right call about whether he needed to see a doctor or go to hospital or whether to watch and wait. It makes it even harder when your loved one is insisting they don't want to call anyone in case they end up in hospital.

Nick caught norovirus one winter and in a matter of 3 hours went from seemingly 'well' to being very ill indeed. By the time I got him to hospital his vision was extremely blurred, he could hardly walk and was very weak. He was in hospital for over a week with a catheter attached to his stoma bag to cope with the diarrhoea and on constant fluids as well as antibiotics. I learnt to act quickly when he had vomiting or diarrhoea.

Another time Nick went from being a bit quiet and under the weather to very quickly being delirious, hallucinating and scaring the heck out of me. I didn't know what was wrong. I knew an infection could cause someone to act very strangely and out of character but I was also concerned that the problem was being caused by the brain tumour he had developed by this time. I remember him getting up and saying he was hungry and eating more than he had eaten in days at one meal, eating fast and furiously while laughing about random things. Could he have an infection when his appetite was suddenly so huge? But I knew something was very wrong so I called the hospice, they advised I call 111, a doctor was sent out to see Nick, but taking about 5 worrying hours to arrive, and he advised I got him to hospital quickly.

The symptoms Nick got with his infections were not always the kind of symptoms I was used to. Pre cancer I had no idea that a fall in temperature could be a sign that an infection may be brewing. I didn't know that changes in behaviour, or hallucinations that came on so quickly, could be a sign. Fever, yes, vomiting and diarrhoea yes but a nasty infection can manifest in so many more ways.

Things we learnt:

- An accurate thermometer is very useful.
- A fall in temperature may be (but isn't always) a sign of infection brewing and should be watched.
- It can take a while to determine what the infection actually is as cultures are often needed etc. but doctors often use broad spectrum antibiotics until they have identified the infection and can treat with targeted medication.
- Trust your instinct and seek medical advice quickly, whatever the patient says

Scans

Suzanna

Mark had several scans during his illness, with the first CAT scan being the diagnosis of cancer. This was followed by an emergency scan when he collapsed and they found he had pulmonary embolisms. So, to us, scans were already a very daunting, scary event and the post chemo scans were especially nerve wracking.

Mark's first post treatment scan was done after his second cycle of chemo. We were both very nervous about it. I can remember having dreadful butterflies, waiting for the results. On the Macmillan site, we used to call the wait 'scanxiety ' and would support each other through it on line. We would then congratulate or commiserate over the results.

Generally patients have the scan, then wait to see their oncologist later for the results. It was a very tense time for us, but as Mark's symptoms had improved dramatically with chemo, we were hoping for good news. Result day arrived and my online friends wished us good luck. Our community Macmillan Nurse phoned, to wish us well, saying she would pop in the next day for an update and to see how Mark was. Hopefully sharing in our good news.

When we saw Mark's oncologist, we were greeted with a "Wow, look at you!". No oxygen and no wheelchair had him amazed. He said it would be no surprise to us to hear, as the improvement showed, the primary tumour had shrunk and the mets had not grown or spread any further. We were delighted ... yes.... the chemo had worked. We were urged on by these results and Mark was keen to have more chemo, to see if it could possibly shrink the tumours further.

I went online to let my friends on the Macmillan site know our good news, but paused for a while, thinking of the poor people that may have recently had bad news and would my news be hurtful to them? I noticed another member had had good scan results too and said she felt bad posting it, but other members had said "no don't feel bad, we love to hear good news, it lifts us up", so I added my news and everyone was so pleased for us. Our Macmillan and District Nurses were delighted too and for a while we basked in the warm glow of our reprieve from symptoms, support of family, friends and Nurses and a better time for Mark.

Mark's second post treatment scan was done when he had completed all four chemo cycles. This time, despite our hopes of more shrinkage, there had been none, but no growth either. The tumours were exactly the same size as at the last scan, two chemo cycles earlier. Little niggly worries crept into my mind, he had endured two more gruelling sessions, to no avail. Could this mean his cancer had become resistant to chemo and started to fight back, taking over his body once more? A very upsetting thought and I really hoped I was wrong.

Mark was now swopped onto maintenance chemo, as full chemo had finished. The idea of maintenance was hopefully to keep any shrinkage at bay. I prayed he could just stay at the stage he was at, it would buy him more time. What we really didn't want was for the cancer to become active again and regrow.

Sadly, the maintenance chemo did absolutely nothing and all of his previous symptoms returned. The headaches were back with a vengeance, he was breathless again, new lumps appeared in his neck and chest, and he became very unwell. Mark was admitted into Hospital and I was filled with anxiety. I knew all of these signs meant a re-awakening of the dreaded disease, he needed oxygen again and constant pain relief. The signs were not good, his health was declining rapidly.

Mark had what was to be his last scan as an in-patient. When the Doctor came onto the ward, with his results, we were told it was bad news. The tumours were growing rapidly. This was the worst news possible and it hit home hard. We were reeling and devastated, both of us in tears.
We asked to go home and were allowed, with both District Nurses and Community Macmillan support. We were given an appointment to see the oncologist to discuss any options for further treatment that may be possible, at this late stage. All we wanted was to get out of there and escape the news, as if by leaving we could leave it all behind; oh if only that were possible, we would run for the hills. But no, home was where we needed to be.

Lara

Scanxiety says it all. Scans can have you watching the radiology staff for a sign of what they have seen and holding your breath for days wondering about what news they will bring.

As Nick and I saw it they could bring bad, good or excellent news. Bad if new activity was found, larger tumours or new tumours. Good if things remained stable and excellent if there was a reduction in the size or number of tumours. Others may see scan results differently, if they have a possibility to be cancer free, but for us with Nick's incurable diagnosis that was how we saw the results. He had many types of scan; CT scans, MRI scans, ultrasounds and nuclear scans.

At first scans were very straightforward but then Nick developed an allergy to the contrast dye they needed to use for a good image. So steroids had to be taken several times before each MRI scan, starting 24 hours before the appointment. Once when he developed breathing problems the radiographer refused to carry out the requested scan as he hadn't had the steroids so we were sent home and the next day he had a nuclear scan as the MRI machine was fully booked. He was found to have multiple clots in both lungs – and we'd been sent home!

As usual Nick was far calmer than I about the scans. He said the results would be the same whether he stressed or not. Goodness I wish I could have been so calm. I would sleep very poorly the night before results or for more nights if I felt the signs weren't good. I braced myself as we entered the doctor's room and took a deep breath in. Normally we knew before we were told. A "Hello, how are you feeling today?" start to the conversation often meant bad news was to follow, a "Wonderful, please sit down" was followed by excellent news. I don't remember once getting good news as Nick's cancer was always on the advance or on retreat.

The one part of his body that was never scanned during this time was his head. I don't know whether that was a good or bad thing but when Nick couldn't use one side of his body properly one day and over the next few days it got worse and worse and other things were being affected we didn't need an image to guess that the cancer had spread to his brain. A scan confirmed this and was probably the most upsetting scan result that Nick ever got. I didn't want to think of cancer growing there.

There is something about the helplessness you feel while waiting for results from scans that is very difficult to deal with. Where symptom changes can make you think that treatment is working or not working on your loved ones cancer, a scan is the absolute proof of that. You have nowhere to hide from scan results, no burying your head in the sand. Scanxiety, as I said at the start, says it all.

Medication

Suzanna

I learnt all of Mark's medications off by heart. The names of drugs, their dosage, what they were for, and why he needed them. He already suffered from angina and had been fitted with a stent 7 years earlier, so he was on medication to stop him from having any further heart problems and keep him well. Suddenly needing cancer drugs on top made for a lot of medication.

If I was going to become responsible for medicating him, it was majorly important for me to be on the ball. I needed to know exactly what tablets I was giving him and be spot on with both dosage and timing. He was a very sick man and there was absolutely no margin for error.

Mark was on a really large cocktail of medication and his prescriptions were constantly changing. I found myself frequently running backwards and forwards to an increasingly concerned chemist, but I was on top of it. I took every single leaflet out of every single box and read it thoroughly. I then kept a log of drugs and memorised their names and effects. I also kept a diary showing when each medication needed to be re-ordered, when to alter doses or change medications and the timings. A few days before chemo extra drugs were needed to prepare for treatment, steroids being the main one.

We had District Nurses coming in to give daily blood thinning injections, as Mark already had blood clots on his lungs. Clots are a possible side effect of some chemo, so they needed to keep his blood thinned. He also had a syringe driver continually administering anti sickness drugs and this needed replenishing daily. Mark had been horrendously sick and there was no let up from it. As Mark was oxygen dependant, he needed to travel to appointments by ambulance. He was once so sick in the ambulance, en route for a check-up that they had to take it off the road and have it cleaned. With him being so run down and weak, he needed the anti-sickness drugs, otherwise all of his medications kept coming back up, as well as any food we managed to get down him. Luckily the syringe driver was a massive help and the sickness subsided.

The Nurses became part of our daily routine. I knew them all by name, feeling it was only manners to learn them as they were spending so much time with us. Sometimes they visiting twice daily; to top up the syringe driver and give his blood thinning injection in the morning and then to check the driver was functioning properly at night. The batteries needed changing regularly too, there was a reading on the pump to tell you how much power was left in the batteries and if under a certain level, they were changed. We even went and bought some to help out. The site of the syringe driver needle needed changing often as it became very sore after a few days. It was positioned at different points on his body and as soon as it became swollen or inflamed it was moved elsewhere.

This became the norm and a daily routine for us. It's amazing how quickly you can adjust to a whole new way of life if you need to. I was extremely focused and very aware of the enormity of my role as a carer and a medicator.

Lara

Over the years the number of meds Nick had to take increased considerably. At first, with his initial course of chemo we took home some anti-nausea meds, a few days' worth of steroids, and very little else. Towards the end I would have a member of staff from our local pharmacy help me carry the boxes of prescribed pills, liquid medicines, daily injections, skin creams, mouth rinses, nasal sprays, high calorie drinks and protein jellies out to the car along with the distilled water for the oxygen concentrator.

Nick wanted to keep control of his life as much as he could and one of the things he did was organise his medication. He knew which meds to take at what time, what couldn't be taken together and what should be taken before or after food. He took his first tablets of the day half an hour before breakfast and his last just before he went to sleep at night.

I learnt what was what and would look for reactions when any new medications were added to the list. There was once when the skin on his neck and chest went bright red and started peeling off. It was very painful and that happened after he had been given an injection to stop the severe stomach spasms and cramps he was getting with chemo. After that he refused the injection and the problem, once healed, never recurred. Linking in new side effects with new medication or changes in dose of existing medication helped on a number of occasions.

He found the easiest way to remember his medication was to put the majority of tablets into a pill box so we bought a large box with 4 compartments for each day of the week and I would help him fill it once a week. We also had a print out of all his medication and what should be taken when, that served as a really useful check list. We also carried the list with us when we were out of the house, never knowing when it might be useful.

When admitted to hospital we had to take all his medication with him in the original packages but it got to the stage that I was carrying 2 bags of medication as well as his suitcase so he decided to just take along his pill box for most of his meds and then he had to sign a disclaimer saying that he accepted responsibility for administering them himself. The staff quickly realised that we knew his meds inside out and were happy for him to do that.

It was impossible to put in one repeat prescription for everything at once as Nick was prescribed different meds for different lengths of time and new meds were added and old meds taken out at all sorts of times so I became a regular at our local pharmacy, usually visiting at least twice a week. The staff there were fantastic and extremely helpful. In fact it was them who told me after about the first 4 or 5 months that Nick probably didn't need to be paying for his prescriptions.

I had taken yet another prescription in and when the medications were given to me the pharmacist took me to one side and said "I don't know exactly what your husband has but it must be something serious and I think you should be getting your prescriptions free of charge. I'd check with his GP if I were you". I thanked him and on checking with the GP was told yes he was. When asked why they hadn't told us that they said it wasn't their job to tell us. I'm still not sure whose job they thought it was, thank goodness for a helpful and kind pharmacist as it saved us a small fortune.

Something else we found out by asking was that many of the medicines Nick was taking were available in liquid form.

There were times when he had problems swallowing tablets and being able to take most of his meds in liquid form was a huge help.

We also found that if one medication doesn't suit or work there are plenty of others that can be tried. Different anti-nausea meds, different meds for mouth ulceration, different pain relief. So if something wasn't doing its job, or the side effects were very unpleasant, new meds were tried until the most effective was found.

When Nick got to the hospice they gently let him know that he didn't need his medication anymore or the daily blood thinning injections, just the pain relief. I think it was a huge relief to him after so long on so much medication. It had done the job for a long while, for which we were extremely grateful but it was time to stop, they no longer served a purpose.

Things we learnt

- Remember to look after yourself too! If you need medications yourself, don't forget to collect them and take them.
- If you feel ill see a Doctor. It's important to stay well in order to care for your loved one.
- You are entitled to a free flu jab as a carer, because you can't afford to be ill, or to pass it on to the patient.
- Make sure you never run out of any medication, I found a log of medications, together with dates to re order, very helpful. Leaving enough time for the prescription to be written to avoid last minute stress.

- It's good to know the names of meds and what they are used for.
- Store drugs carefully especially controlled drugs like morphine, or needles, keep well away from children.
- I found locking drugs and needles away to prevent any accidents was the safest option. Especially as I have several Grandchildren.
- Cancer patients are entitled to free prescriptions, they just need an exemption form from their GP.

Out of hours

Suzanna

It can be very difficult to get help out of hours. Our Macmillan Nurses only worked 9 to 5 on week days, so were not reachable outside these hours. If you phone for a Doctor out of hours you get a Locum, with no idea of the patient's case history. But we were very lucky in that we had District Nurses too and they worked every day, all week and also evenings, up to a certain time. Obviously they didn't work through the night though so we were given a number to ring if we needed them. They were calling daily at one point anyway, Mark was very ill from the onset and we needed their support. As the chemo kicked in and he improved the visits did drop down.

There was one Sunday when the District Nurse decided Mark needed a Doctor out. It was a locum and we waited ages for him to come. He left a prescription for steroids, anti-sickness meds, needles and anti-biotics but on a Sunday open chemists are scarce and, as I could neither drive nor leave Mark, I struggled to get the medication. I had to ring around family to see who was available to fetch it for us and in the end my sister went and she had quite a drive to find a chemist who actually had the medication in stock at the time.

We were also given a number for the chemo ward to ring in an emergency for advice, so on the whole we were far luckier than many cancer patients. I did have to ring in a couple of times when Mark was actively having treatment and our district nurse rang them for advice too. It's good to have somewhere to turn to when needed as its scary enough coping with all the eventualities of cancer, without having any backup plan around you.

There was only the very odd occasion when I wasn't sure what to do. As I'm not a Nurse I struggled to gauge what was urgent and what could wait. But as soon as the District Nurse arrived, she knew and would generally say, "Let's get the Doctor out", or "I will ring the cancer ward". This took the pressure off me and Mark couldn't really argue with her decision, as much as he didn't like a fuss. If the Nurse said a Doctor was needed then a Doctor it was, whereas if I suggested it, Mark would say "NO, I am ok".

I was very glad of the support on many occasions and the relief of not having that decision to make and the ensuing battle with Mark, to allow me to send for help. As ill as he was, he could still let me know if he didn't want me to call anyone.

The night he collapsed with pulmonary embolisms, he was still insisting I didn't ring for help but he was ashen and gasping for breath, so even I knew it was necessary to overrule him. On that occasion it was a 999 call, as it was the middle of the night and help was needed urgently. When the ambulance arrived they said I had done exactly the right thing as he was close to death by that time and needed clot busting drugs in order to survive. He hadn't even started chemo then, so a collapse before treatment could have ruled out the chance of any chemo whatsoever, an awful predicament. **In time I learnt to trust my gut instinct and overrule Mark as necessary.**

Lara

One subject that cropped up many times on the Macmillan Carers Group in the online forum was what to do if your loved one seemed unwell out of hours.   Carers want the best for their loved one with cancer but don't want to bother the stretched medical services unnecessarily.   Also they were often being told by their loved one not to call.

There were times when Nick was at home and became unwell or just "wasn't right" when I felt completely overwhelmed with the responsibility of what to do. How ill was he? Was I being paranoid? Should we wait and watch or seek medical help straight away?

In the early days after diagnosis when treatment was new it was possible to overreact, but better this than ignore something that could need medical attention. As time passed and he became weaker he became more susceptible to infections and developed a number of allergies that possibly would have been fatal if ignored. In the late stages he really didn't want to go to hospital and would underplay things which of course I understood but then I couldn't bear to think of him suffering.

There were occasions when it was obvious that he needed medical attention; a serious bleed from around his stoma that we couldn't stop or vomiting and diarrhoea which was dangerous with an ileostomy as dehydration can occur very rapidly. A high temperature (or a low temperature) needed checking out as did anything from a weeping abscess to delirium.

There were other times when it wasn't clear cut. One day I noticed Nick was breathing differently as he sat down after taking the dog for a short walk. He had recently started a course of chemotherapy with a new cocktail of drugs. Had he just over done it, was he having some reaction? He said he'd be fine and would just lie down and have a nap. After climbing the stairs to the bedroom he sounded even more short of breath.

Instinct is an important sense and one a carer should feel confident to use. We are the ones with our loved one more than anyone else, we notice small changes that other people may miss. Nick really didn't feel like going to hospital as he knew he would be there all day, passed from pillar to post and back again, and sitting around waiting for long periods. He felt rotten and just wanted to sleep. But I was feeling worried and insisted on calling the chemo ward.

Of course they told me to bring him in to the hospital and we were passed from nurse to doctor and back again, in between sitting around waiting. The trouble is, when someone is already ill, with lung metastases along with everything else it can be hard to judge when something other than the cancer is causing a problem. So after listening to his chest and making him walk up and down stairs while monitoring his breathing and his pulse they felt there was nothing much to be concerned about. Thankfully the super-thorough chemotherapy ward doctor decided she wanted to do a scan of his chest, to be on the safe side.

We were sent to another part of the hospital for a scan but the radiologist wanted to use a contrast dye which Nick had developed an allergy to and he needed steroids before he was able to have a scan. More sitting around while they decided what to do and in the end sent home as they decided on a nuclear scan which didn't need dye which couldn't be carried out until the next morning.

So, home we went and Nick went straight off to bed as he was totally shattered. I felt I had put him through an exhausting day with no result and knew the next day would be the same. It was a restless night for me. Nick slept but when he got up in the night he just sounded wrong, he was breathing faster and it was more shallow than normal. It wasn't a huge difference, but to me it didn't seem right.

The next morning Nick was worn out from just getting dressed and we went off to hospital again for the scan. It was carried out and he was whisked straight into the High Dependency Unit. He had multiple Pulmonary Emboli that the head of nuclear medicine described as "dramatic". I left Nick in hospital, went home to pack a bag for him to take back, and had a mini melt down while I was there. He had multiple clots in his lungs and we'd been sent home. He could have died in the night. The reality of that hit me hard.

There were a number of other occasions when I had to make a call on getting Nick seen by a doctor and I never regretted the decision.

It can be hard enough making the right call during normal working hours. Things become so much harder and scarier at night or at the weekend when you don't know who to contact for help. Dial 111? 999? Call the hospital? Go to Accident and Emergency? Call no-one and just stay up worrying? What do you do when the person you are caring for doesn't want you to call anyone but you feel that they need attention? It is a mine field and the responsibility of getting it right can feel overwhelming.

I used to read so many posts in the carers group on the Macmillan Online Community site with scared carers asking just these questions. They didn't want to go against the wishes of their loved one, they didn't want to worry them but felt that they needed medical attention, they didn't want to waste anyone's time. What if it turned out to be nothing? They wondered if they should wait until the morning or Monday and call the GP then. Time after time other carers would respond.

Depending on what the worry was about they would share their own experiences, but above all the message was clear – if in doubt get help or if your instinct tells you something is wrong get help. Some people had a hospital number to call if there were problems, others had to rely on 111 or if the situation seemed serious enough then 999 or drive their loved one to accident and emergency.

Whichever option was taken you knew that there would be waiting and delays if out of hours, more so than normal which I believe is one of the reasons the person with cancer can be so reluctant to go to hospital. As a carer, what you want is someone at the end of a phone as soon as you need them, to talk through a situation, a symptom, a worry. To give you informed advice about the best course of action to take. To come to the house quickly if needed.

This happened as soon as Nick was under the care of our local hospice. If we were concerned about anything, if his breathing was becoming more difficult or the pain was too much to bear or anything else we had a number to call and we knew that he would get the help and support he needed. It was a huge, huge relief. I have no medical training and all I wanted was to know there was someone with that training to turn to 24 hours a day, 7 days a week who would talk me through what to try or arrange to visit or to tell me to call an ambulance. As a carer not only does your loved one often resist going to hospital but you know how busy hospitals and on call doctors are. The last thing we want to do is waste their time but neither do we want to risk our caree suffering. It can be a hard balancing act and a huge responsibility.

We didn't have a district nurse to call on but know that they are a huge comfort and support to many. 111 can be useful but sometimes the delays seem far too long. I think what I learnt was that, as a rule of thumb, it doesn't matter what day it is or what hour it is you can always find help somewhere. I kept a list of useful phone numbers so I never had to waste time searching around for them. Ask the hospital what to do in an emergency or, if you are worried about anything, ask your Macmillan nurse or GP. Knowing where help is makes bearing the responsibility a little easier and a little less daunting.

Visiting Hospital

Suzanna

When Mark's symptoms returned, I knew the cancer was active and on the move again. I just wanted someone to listen to me and acknowledge what I was saying, prove me right, or hopefully wrong. But I felt unheard. One of the doctors was very dismissive, condescending even. It just made everything feel so much worse and I was frustrated at my inability to get my point across. The last thing a carer needs is to be spoken down to, as if they know nothing or are irrelevant.

Many times I came away from hospital visits and appointments feeling I wasn't heard, understood or taken seriously. I feel it's important for medical staff to stay in tune with the carer as well as the patient. Together we are a team and working as such is likely to be beneficial to all.

No one knows the patients better than their primary carer. We are the ones who are at home with them all the time, battling away to look after them under difficult circumstances and noticing changes in symptoms. If we are worried about the patient, we will have good reason to be. By really listening to, and acting on, our worries symptoms may be investigated before a crisis occurs.

Carers deserve respect, we only have the patients' best interests at heart after all. We can also give valuable information about what is happening to the patient, so should be included and kept in the loop. Medical staff could help carers by speaking to us regularly, not leaving us to chase around after staff for an update, when our loved one is in hospital.

Lara

It wasn't just surgery that had Nick staying in hospital for weeks on end. He had a number of infections, norovirus which with an ileostomy can be very serious, and pulmonary embolisms that the doctor described as "dramatic".

Long stays in hospital for a loved one means long days of hospital visits for the carer. These can be both physically and emotionally draining but they can be vital for your loved ones recovery and peace of mind. The focus is obviously on the person in hospital but it can be a difficult and stressful experience for the carer.

Nick was an inpatient at several hospitals. In all of them, without exception, we found the care in the HDU/ICU faultless. The staff were caring, attentive and efficient as well as very professional. On the ward the care was usually equally as good but doctors and nurses are human's not robots and there were mistakes made. Nick was always informed and alert about his care, his medication, and everything in between. This, not me I'm ashamed to say, saved him more than once.

Once a nurse was attempting to give Nick a dose of ketamine that was significantly more than it should have been. Luckily he noticed the measure cup was far fuller than normal. Another time he felt something was wrong and got me to check the syringe driver pumping him with medication. As soon as I saw the name on the driver started with "Mrs" I was out of the door and up to the nurse's station faster than I knew my legs could take me. I returned in a flash with a doctor whose face had visibly lost colour when I told him and who removed the syringe faster than my legs had carried me up the corridor. After those incidents we were even more vigilant, querying and questioning doses and timings of meds. I learnt to trust Nick's instinct so if he said something didn't feel right I'd get it checked. I understand these were accidents and that accidents happen but they could have had devastating outcomes.

Although he was good at keeping calm being in hospital was hard for Nick. Sleep was even worse than usual, he was there for a reason so feeling worse than normal anyway, and he could be moody. This moodiness meant he could appear irritated or just silent and withdrawn. I found both of these hard although they were perfectly understandable. There I was traipsing around London with a bag full of the things that he had requested I bring that day and a few little treats for him, knowing I would spend my day sitting by a bed feeling upset and deeply saddened by what my husband was going through, having conversations interrupted by nurses and physiotherapists and maybe a visit by the consultant.

I tried to keep a smile on my face and look relaxed while keeping Nick entertained when he needed distraction or let him rest and sleep when he needed. It was draining, at times it was frankly boring, but I know he needed me there. It was a comfort for him to have me sit by him and hold his hand or read out clues to the crossword, to ramble away about life outside the hospital walls or to listen when he needed to talk, he depended on me being there each day. We amused ourselves devising all sorts of hospital escape plans, a distraction which began when the window next to his bed in Hospital overlooked a cell block and the walls of the local prison.

And every evening I would go home and make the round of phone calls to update family on how Nick was doing and got used to the fact that I would be asked how he was but rarely how I was. I would fill in the boys honestly but not always fully and I would go to bed alone, tired, scared and restless. Spending all day at the hospital meant that other jobs needed catching up on once home. In one way it was good to be busy but in another it could be hard to find the energy or incentive.

Things we learnt:

- Learn the daily routine at the hospital, ward rounds, daily x-ray timings, meals, etc. and time your visits accordingly.
- Make sure that your loved one has enough nightwear to leave spares at the hospital and take plastic bags to carry dirty laundry home. Hospital gowns are uncomfortable and as soon as they are not needed cosy PJs from home are much more comforting.
- Warm slippers and pairs of bed socks may be helpful if your loved one feels the cold or has peripheral neuropathy.
- Packing a naturally scented spray can be useful. A bit on the dressing gown can help smother hospital scents which aren't always welcome and if your loved one is getting used to a stoma or having to change/empty their stoma bag in bed, a spray of citrus scent can be really helpful at masking the odour for them and others on the ward.
- It can be hard coming up with conversation after a few days, especially on long visits. A crossword or a puzzle book that you can do together will help pass the time and give a focus.
- Pack a few tempting treats and a few drinks for your loved one.

Managing at Home During Treatment

Suzanna

As Mark became very hoarse and hardly able to speak, I found him a little hand bell to ring if he wanted me. Wherever I was in the house, I could hear it and would then go to him to see what he needed. Wife on call literally! It became very helpful, as he could hardly shout me. It also gave Hubby peace of mind that he could get attention easily if needed.

The bell became a laughing point with visitors and family members. Especially my Brother in law, who has a wicked sense of humour and who encouraged Hubby to use it frequently. He even rang it himself, to ask for a cup of tea or waitress service. I began to think my idea was not such a good one after all! But it was all done to lighten the mood and to make Hubby smile, it did raise a few laughs along the way.

It was very useful when only the two of us were at home though. A short sharp ring gained my attention and I went running to him. This was very important at night as the oxygen machine was so loud I couldn't sleep in the same room, besides Hubby needed space to move around and stretch out in. Although sleep was not something either of us had much of.

I seemed to spend most nights listening out for him, his bell, the drone of the oxygen machine , a coughing fit or, the very worst thing of all, too much quiet. Now this had me jumping out of bed to check up on him. I was in the next room and left both doors propped open. My ears were tuned in for his sounds all night every night. I found myself waking and checking him several times throughout the night. His position, his breathing, the oxygen supply, scary stuff. Too many what ifs.

What if he had stopped breathing and I hadn't noticed? What if he had choked? What if I hadn't heard him ring the bell? What if he had an angina attack and couldn't reach his spray, or alert me? All of these things played on my mind constantly. We tried sleeping together, but it really wasn't practical any more, he needed space and peace to sleep in. Not a fidgety wife with hot sweats constantly twitching around him, disturbing him. We decided separate rooms were best and I would keep a close, watchful eye on him.

Nursing Hubby was broad and varied, open ended even, always changing, as his needs altered. I was taught how to give him the blood thinning injections as part of our daily routine as time went on. I was terrified of being too rough and hurting him, his skin was fragile. He gave it to himself for a short while, but he soon became too weak and shaky, so I took over the task .I continually asked him if he was ok, as I nervously plunged the needle into his abdomen and gently squeezed the liquid into his body.

Washing him and keeping his skin moisturised was an important part of his daily care. Nice clean sheets and clothing were a must. Also keeping his strength up with homemade soups and healthy and appropriate meals .Plenty of fluids, rest, not too many visitors, all of these things kept me on my toes.

Lara

For a long time we managed okay at home. There were periods, when chemo was taking its toll on Nick, when recovering from surgery or coping with the side effects of radiotherapy, when the responsibility of looking after him became tough but we managed. Over the years Nick became weaker and more susceptible to infections and side effects. Allergies developed and recovery became harder.

As a wife I often felt helpless. Unable to take away the pain or discomfort, the exhaustion and side effects. But time taught me that just being there, being Nick's constant, gave him comfort and relief, he knew that I would be there by his side.

At night if a panic attack struck or if he needed help with his ileostomy bag or if he just needed to feel the warmth and comfort of someone lying next to him in bed who would watch over him and wake in an instant if I sensed something was needed. The nights I lay listening to his breathing listening for changes. Bubbling from a possible infection or breathing that seemed too slow and sometimes just waiting for the next breath to make sure it came.

I looked for any changes after medications were altered. Would there be a reaction? Would it help? I learnt to calm him during a panic attack although, in truth, I could easily have panicked along side him. I learnt when he needed to clear mucus from his airway and how to help him do this and I would gently bathe him and wash his hair when he was too tired, or unable, to do this for himself.

Managing visitors was something else I could do. Make sure there weren't too many or that they didn't stay too long.

Some people were very considerate and self-managed their visits, keeping them short. Others seem unable to leave even if they could see how tired Nick was and so needed some prompting from me. There were days when, other than walking the dog and making meals, I would spend most of the day just sitting with him watching a box set or sitting quietly by as he dozed. We'd talk about our children, family and friends, about the news and what was happening in the world, about treatment. When he was well we'd pop out for a meal or see friends or potter in the garden if the weather was fine. It was a quiet life, full of simple pleasures, managing his symptoms and togetherness whatever we were doing.

It wasn't until very near the end of his life that Nick would accept any outside help. He wanted me to care for him and I wanted that too although at times I was scared and felt out of my depth. The years of poor quality sleep had caught up with me and my mind was at times sludgy through lack of rest. I was also less fit from eating badly, gaining weight and not getting nearly as much exercise as previously making it harder to keep up with all that needed doing. We also had a serious worry with one of our children and Nick didn't have the capacity left to deal with it so that fell on my shoulders too as did the trauma of a very close family member being diagnosed with cancer at a young age. Carers often have more than just one person in their lives needing support.

The involvement of the hospice nurses was invaluable and made me feel relieved that I didn't have to manage everything alone any more. They were there at the end of the phone line. After having so many big scares over time it was such a comfort to have their knowledge and experience there as back up and they were a calm and helpful background presence which was invaluable to us both.

Mealtimes and Food

Suzanna

Food became a daily battle as Mark's appetite was erratic. He had nodules in his throat and windpipe, making it difficult to swallow his own saliva sometimes, let alone food.

Chemo left him with both mouth ulcers and thrush at the same time, he was run down, in a lot of pain and miserable. Our community Mac Nurse ran me to the chemist to pick up a prescription to treat thrush and a mouthwash for ulcers. It continued for several days and she popped in the following week to check on him. He had also been vomiting continually and needed a syringe driver to administer constant anti sickness drugs.

He kept saying food had no taste, was very bland, but the smell would have him heaving. As his taste buds failed him, his sense of smell elevated to a point of turning his stomach at the drop of a hat. He tolerated instant porridge well and we had a copious amount in the cupboard. Homemade soups were also a favourite. Blended to a pulp, it was easy to swallow and digest. Vegetable soups became a must, nutritious as possible and they slid down a treat. Sometimes a casserole was tolerated.

He developed a taste for puddings, sponge and custard being his preference, yoghurts and ice cream, anything sweet. The occasional cream doughnut, soft and full of calories was eaten. I didn't mind what he ate, as long as he ate something and kept it down. The district nurse told me to add skimmed milk powder to puddings, soups and stews to bump up the calorie intake. When he couldn't eat at all the fruity fortisip juices, on prescription, helped keep his liquid and vitamin levels up.

The days he was on steroids pre-treatment boosted his appetite and he ate fairly well. But on the days when he ate almost nothing, I really worried and tried desperately to tempt him with anything at all. If he fancied it, I would obtain it and prepare it for him, in the hope he would keep it down. Hubby's eating habits became a big issue and I spent a lot of time planning meals and preparing them, sometimes to be rejected as he really couldn't face it. When he actually enjoyed a meal I was delighted, but the times this happened was very few and far between.

Lara

With the help of anti-sickness meds Nick managed to eat fairly well for some time after diagnosis, even during chemotherapy, but cancer and food are often not an easy combination. Gradually out went the weekly shops and the meal planning, in came last minute dashes to the supermarket, fingers crossed that they would have in stock the one thing he felt like eating that day. As the medication increased so did the number of possible reactions with certain foods (e.g. grapefruit) and supplements. Nick always checked with the doctor and pharmacist and several times was advised to cut out certain supplements while on a particular medication.

The first year, even two years, weren't so bad. Yes there were days in the chemo cycle when certain foods or smells would turn his stomach but there were other days in the cycle when he still felt like a home cooked curry and dhal or a fish pie. Enjoyment of a glass of wine vanished never to return but he didn't seem to be losing weight which always felt like a little win against the disease.

Nick had the physique of a racing snake before his diagnosis. He had never been over weight, ate healthily ran nearly every day and practiced Pilates. When you start from a position of no extra padding I felt it was even more important to try and maintain the weight he had.

Something we had always enjoyed doing together was cooking and with more time on his hands, if he had the energy, Nick would cook with me or cook a meal for the family. Cooking on his own led to some "interesting" meals. He had the will to cook and the skill but unfortunately he had never been one for following a recipe. This worked fine until chemo took away or altered his sense of taste. There were a number of occasions when we sat down to a meal he had cooked and as he started happily tucking in the boys and I sat there pulling faces at each other waiting to see who would be the first to comment or laugh. Nick started growing vegetables in the garden so we had a fair bit of organic home grown food. Most of it appreciated by us all though I'm not sure our boys will want to eat another courgette or kale for many years to come.

There were a number of things which affected Nick's appetite and ability to eat; chemo, surgery, his ileostomy, radiotherapy, and the final months of life.

During the early courses of chemo he managed pretty well. Food tasted different and there was the constant battle with oral thrush but he ate. Oriental food became a no-no for some reason but a mild curry was still okay. Textures became as important as flavours – nothing too chewy, nothing stodgy, nothing gloopy, nothing that would stick in the throat on the way down. One day all he felt like was eggs the next it was the last thing he felt like. We were told that it was more important that he ate than what he ate but Nick had never been one for sweet food or fattening food. Quite early on he was given a prescription for high calorie drinks and although he really didn't like them he had them.

When someone is on chemo their appetite can be affected but calorie intake is important. It was a really difficult balancing act, finding something that Nick could face eating and encouraging him to consume a reasonable number of calories. Many of the meals he had loved he could no longer face and I could see him look with dread if a big plate of food was put in front of him. I stopped doing a big weekly shop and bought food most days to suit Nick's taste buds and appetite. Cooking was something we had always done together when we could, so still did if he felt up to it and could cope with the kitchen odours. Occasionally he cooked alone, for all of us. That was when we looked at the food with dread! The change in his taste buds led to some very interesting meals and at least one that was totally inedible for the rest of us. We laughed about it. We laughed about a lot of things. Our sense of humour got darker but we certainly didn't lose it.

I soon learnt that small and often was much better than a big plate of food. Small portions seemed less daunting and do-able and, as time went on, I had to learn to accept that sometimes he just wasn't able to face more than half a sandwich if that. So I would try and ensure that he was drinking plenty of fluids and to leave it at that. One type of chemo, the last he had, made his mouth and throat ulcer terribly. It was incredibly painful to start with let alone when trying to swallow food or drink. The priority then was treating the ulceration as every medication the doctor tried to line the mouth and throat or numb them proved ineffective. That was a horridly upsetting time.

Post operations his appetite would drop off completely and that, combined with hospital food which wasn't always what he could face, meant weight loss. I would try and take food into hospital and when he got home it would be my mission to regain lost ground on the weight front. For hospital I made soups, sometimes with added cream and protein powder, small sandwiches with fillings I knew he enjoyed, took dark chocolate and a few biscuits, bananas.

After his first course of chemo Nick had an operation to remove his primary tumour which left him with an ileostomy. A stoma in the small intestine where anything he ate left his body and was excreted into a stoma bag covering the stoma. With an ileostomy came new food challenges. There were foods that made the "output" too solid, food that caused too much air or gas (never a good thing with a bag of poo stuck on your stomach), food that could block the stoma and, as he was only using his small intestine, fewer nutrients and goodness were being absorbed from the food he ate so in order to get a balanced diet eating became even more important. Drinks and liquid intake became more important too as you can become dehydrated very rapidly if you have an ileostomy.

Another difficult time was after a course of radiotherapy which effected his ability to swallow. The side effects of radiotherapy are cumulative and get worse the longer the radiotherapy continues and then up to three weeks after treatment before beginning to subside. Again it was a period of a liquid diet and a diet of food that was smooth to swallow; soup, scrambled egg, mashed potato, yogurt, mashed banana, smoothies.

For the final months and weeks of life the situation for a carer around food can become very painful. Accepting that the person you love no longer wants to eat is hard to accept and the temptation can be to carry on trying to tempt your loved one with this and that. In order to live people have to eat, and accepting their total loss of interest in food or their increased difficulty with eating anything is, at this stage, accepting that their life is coming to a close.

I think it took being in the hospice to help me accept that food was no longer important. When Nick, while in hospital, decided to end treatment he was given two to three months to live. In the end he lived less than two weeks. He was transferred to the hospice as he didn't want to stay in hospital and didn't want to die at home.

The hospice was wonderful in all respects including their handling of food. The first meal he asked for some soup and a little ice cream. The food came in very small portions as he had asked but he still hardly touched a thing. The hospice staff never pushed him to eat, if he said he wanted no food that was fine, drinks were always available and he continued to sip tea and water. I found his refusal of food so hard to accept. I wanted, needed, those two to three months with him but in my heart I knew I wouldn't get them. The calm and accepting attitude of the hospice helped me be calm and accepting. He had his last cup of tea the evening of the day before he died.

Things we learnt:

- Try not to make food an issue.
- Small portions are best as a large plate full can put them off.
- Go with whatever they fancy as chemo can leave them with strange tastes.
- Freeze batches of soups or casseroles up and thaw as desired.
- If they really can't face food don't push it, let them be.
- There is a lot of advice about diet for cancer sufferers but very little evidence that restricting your diet is helpful. Every person has to do what they think best and the carer has to try and support them with their choices.
- If the person with cancer is considering making big changes to their diet it is worth discussing this with their medical team.
- Certain foods and supplements can react with some medications therefore it is always sensible to check this with their doctor or pharmacist.
- Shop often to avoid waste.
- Many hospitals have dieticians who can advise on nutritional intake.
- If recommended a high protein diet, there are options such as prescription protein jellies and drinks, protein powder or high protein yogurts from the supermarket which can help.

From Spouse to Carer

Suzanna

I don't think people really 'get ' what caring for a loved one who is terminally ill is like, unless they have done it themselves and it is hard to describe. It's all consuming, you are swallowed up by it and almost lose yourself, becoming an extension of the patient.   I was always worrying over Mark's eating, yet would forgot to eat myself. The same with his medication, I was obsessed with his drugs, timing, dosage etc., but forgot I needed to take blood pressure tablets myself.

It's like living in a bubble. Making sure the house is clean and tidy, Hubby gets washed and changed, fed and medicated, then spend the day waiting for nurses, visitors, phone calls, post, more cleaning. It is as if the outside world still exists but you don't really feel a part of it any more, it's surreal. Hospital visits, chemo and its after effects, were a whole new world. Hubby had a complete personality change and suddenly you are living with a stranger after 37 years of marriage. Who is this Man? You grieve for the Husband you had; the capable, placid, dependable man, who loves you, cares for you, keeps you calm, fixes everything, pays the bills, and is constantly on the go doing jobs around the home.

Suddenly he became someone who sat still all day, staring into space , could barely climb the stairs , struggled to breathe, wouldn't talk, became very depressed and snappy, deteriorating rapidly. It is heart breaking, but you have to keep going, for him, for you, the family, everyone.

I focused on looking after him and looking out for him. His voice was hoarse, so I became his voice. I was very possessive over him, he was 'my ' Man, my responsibility and I fought off any competition for his care. Even though sometimes I felt lonely and isolated, I only let visitors in for short periods and then they had to be pre -booked. He tired easily and I could see he couldn't cope with people for long. As soon as I saw him struggle, I asked them to leave. I guess I was border line rude, but I didn't care, he was all that mattered to me at the time. I was driven and on automatic pilot, I only had one mission in life, to care for him and to do it well. I left work, to be by his side constantly. "In sickness and health", those were our vows and I intended to carry them through regardless.

I have to say at this point, we had wonderful support, from both District and Macmillan Nurses, they kept me grounded. I'm sure without them I wouldn't have coped. I will always be grateful to them for their input. Family did try, but I was touchy, struggling and very easily upset. They meant well, but nothing could put right what was happening to us and I couldn't be pacified by anything. My Husband was going to die and soon, how could anything they said or did change the inevitable .They took the backlash of my anger and frustration and forgave me, they knew my pain was deep and crushing .

My Friends were treading on eggshells too, scared to say or do the wrong things and get a tongue lashing. Some backed off, my closest friends rode the storm that was my heartache, knowing I would not be my usual self. Some feared I would crack under the strain but I wouldn't, and I didn't. I knew it was sink or swim time and I wasn't about to sink. Even if it took all of my energy to stay afloat I would do it. Hubby was strong, and I would be strong beside him.

I had the sense to ask for help, counselling firstly, then after Hubby's death, anti-depressants, to stop me falling down like a house of cards. I had tried to imagine what it would be like to lose him, to be a widow, to prepare myself, but I couldn't do it, it was way too painful. I knew it would happen, I would have to face it and that life without him would never be the same. He was my rock, my soul mate, my other half. No this could not be real, it must be a dream an ongoing nightmare. Mark became distant, he wouldn't or couldn't talk to me, share his feelings and that hurt a lot. I so wanted to support him, listen to his fears, but he didn't want to discuss death and shut me out. In his mind he was going to carry on living a lot longer than he actually did. When he became really ill, I was there to comfort him and let him know he wasn't alone. I was there by his side where I belonged and where I would be for as long as he needed me.

Lara

I had a problem with the term "carer". I was a life partner doing what I could to look after my husband through an awful illness. His spouse not his carer.

Carers were, in my mind at that time, people who were paid a meagre sum for doing a very important and valuable job, looking after the practical and personal needs of their clients. They looked after the client while they were at work and, hopefully, were able to switch off at the end of their shift. As a spouse or partner there is little chance to switch off, you're not only dealing with the practical and personal needs of our loved one but you are also nursing them and supporting them emotionally while trying to manage your own emotions and needs. We don't just care for them we also care about them, more than anyone else in the world.

I didn't identify myself as a "carer" and I wasn't identified by anyone else either. No-one told me that as a carer I had rights, that I was entitled to a carer's assessment by my local council, that I could claim a carer's allowance, or that there were support groups I could join. I know I was not the only one. It was finding the Macmillan online forum that made me realise that in order to access support I had to think of myself as, and call myself, a carer however inadequate and incorrect the term felt. I still feel that another title would be more appropriate and more acceptable but I'm not sure what that title would be.

So I became my husband's carer and as time went on sometimes it became hard to remember that I was also his wife and his friend. Caring for him alone until the last few days of his life took over my life and there was more and more that he relied on me for. At times the only way to cope was to shut down emotionally and I just functioned. There were times when I was terrified, when he was choking, when I couldn't stem the flow of blood from his stoma, when he was delirious, when he had a panic attack. I could have panicked with him, I could have cried, screamed even, but I didn't. I switched onto automatic pilot, switched off the emotions and got on with dealing with the situation as well as I could. Did that make me less of a wife and more of a carer? I did wonder sometimes. Although when helping him I did it without feeling, after the event the adrenalin left my system, and I felt it with my whole body and mind. Being a carer doesn't stop you being what you were before the role was forced on you. It is really important to remember that and to hold onto that thought. It needn't end the relationship you had, it changes it. It is your past, the memories, shared life and love that make you see it through.

It is also a reason to ask for outside help and support. From family, friends, carers. If you allow someone else to do the "caring" for a while it gives you some space. Space for yourself and for your relationship. Being at your loved ones side and supporting them through the toughest of times can be mixed. At times you may feel hopeless that there is nothing you can do and you question everything and ask if you could do it better, differently, if you made a right decision. Then at other times you realise you have made a huge difference and that without you walking the cancer path with them things would have been so much harder for your loved one. I will never forget how moved I was when a doctor was asking Nick about his panic attacks, which started when he his breathing problems worsened, and what techniques helped him deal with them. He looked at the doctor and said "I have Lara, she stops them" and reached a hand out to me. My heart burst at that moment and the tears welled up. Yes we are carers, but we are so, so much more as well.

Support

Suzanna

When Mark was diagnosed with lung cancer, we had a very good support network around us. I was offered a carers assessment, but as I had plenty of support already, I felt I really didn't need it. If I had needed it, I would have accepted it readily. Family, friends and Nurses all helped us to get through an incredibly sad and difficult time. Our Son's and partners visited frequently, to keep our spirits up and offer practical support; lifts, odd jobs around the house that Mark would normally do, meals together, wrapping us in a warm blanket of love and keeping a very close eye on us. Our Nurses were also on hand constantly, giving daily injections and checking on us. The whole extended Family stepped in to be there for us when we needed them most. I sometimes feel I wasn't as grateful as I should have been, as I was so wrapped up in Hubby's illness, always distracted by thinking about what comes next.

A very close friend took me early morning shopping, as I don't drive. When I could no longer leave Mark alone, a dear neighbour fetched prescriptions etc. for us. Everyone rallied around. My older Sister made batches of lovely homemade soup for him when he struggled to eat and was always at the end of the phone for me to talk to, providing a sympathetic, listening ear. My Brother helped me with everything financial and accompanied me to important appointments at banks etc. when I needed support (which was frequently). My younger Sister flew over from Spain, where she lives, several times, to be by my side when I needed her. Mark's twin Sister visited regularly and sat with him when I needed to go out for any reason. We were the perfect tag team.

I have to say we were very lucky regarding support. But I am also aware this is not the case for everyone. Nursing for instance can be a bit of a postcode lottery and not all areas have Macmillan Nurses. Also some people do not have close family to turn to for support, as they either don't have any, or they live too far away.

Occasionally there can be a rift between families, this is even more unfortunate and distressing at such times. Sometimes the rift can be healed and relationships repaired , as the whole situation brings people to their senses , realising what's really important , to pull together united as a family should be , burying the hatchet, forgiving and forgetting past grudges . Sometimes, sadly, rifts are not healed, as things have gone way too far and are now beyond repair. This deprives families of the support they need so much and is very sad indeed.

There can also be times when there is a clash between family's wishes, where they have conflicting ideas of how and where the patient should be treated. This can cause dreadful arguments, where hurtful words are spoken in the heat of the moment causing irreparable damage, from which there is no turning back. Tempers become frayed and the situation is fraught.

Sadly there have been occasions such as this mentioned on the Macmillan community site. Carers were desperately trying to sort out family feuds and differences of opinions, on top of caring for their loved ones. This is where a support group can be very helpful indeed. It is somewhere to turn to, when you are feeling so very alone, troubled and desperate for support. Gentle advice and ideas of how to cope, given sympathetically from other carers, who know exactly how you feel, is a valuable source of support at times like this. Occasionally such support can give a response that could resolve the problem and restore family harmony. An outsider can provide an open and unbiased view, adding a whole new angle to the situation, one that the carer may not have thought of. Sometimes it might actually work, but at the very least be worth a try.

Things We Learnt

- Make the most of any support offered to you.
- You are entitled to a carer's assessment, to see how much support you actually qualify for.
- Accept offers of help graciously, even if just to give yourself a breather. A short walk, a coffee with friends and a chat, can make you feel much better.
- The patient may be glad of the break, someone else to talk to, a change of face, can be good for them too.
- A community support site can be an enormous source of support.
- Unfortunately not everyone gets the support they need and deserve. There is support to be found; the Macmillan helpline, your GP, at the hospital, hospice, online or a local carers group.
- Hospices and hospitals have palliative care teams.

Macmillan Online Community

Suzanna

The Macmillan Online Community is a support group which allows anyone who has been affected by Cancer to join their community site. You will then have contact with people who are going through the same experiences as you are and will understand what you are going through. Members of the community give each other support and advice. It's a place to make friends and voice your troubles and emotions to people that never judge you, they just listen and support you. Sometimes laughing together, often crying together, but together none the less, no matter what time of day or night, there is always someone around to answer your posts.

A complete Godsend to many and a clever way to stay in contact with the outside world that seems to continue to move on regardless of anyone's plight. It helps you to realise that you are not alone on this journey, in fact there are many others travelling the same path as you. Staying in touch can help to keep you grounded, knowing that others are beside you all the way. You can compare notes, experiences and stages with them, give each other advice on which techniques worked for you and tips to help ailments.

There are different groups for different types of cancer, a group for carers, families, the bereaved, everything is catered for. You simply join the groups that are relevant to you on your individual journey. There are also admin, moderators and community champions to guide you on your way. A totally brilliant idea and a thriving community of likeminded people. If you don't wish to post comments, you can just read the posts of others. That way you can pick up tips and advice.

If you are looking for anything specific, just type it into the search bar and any relevant replies will appear. I personally found this very helpful at many stages throughout Mark's illness and after he sadly died.

I made many online friends during Hubby's illness, at carers only group, I had a massive amount of advice and support through some of the darkest months of my life, from some very wise and experienced carers. I had people to turn to, to share my troubles with and to listen to theirs and came away with sound advice time and time again, who better to talk to a carer than another carer? Sometimes you would get several replies to a post with a range of suggestions and helpful advice. If you had been through an awful experience or your loved one was in hospital there was always someone there to ask how your day was and to show an interest in your troubles. This sort of support is priceless.

When Hubby sadly died I swopped over to the bereaved spouses and partners group. They were especially supportive and comforting. It was good to be able to talk to people who knew what I was going through and exactly how I was feeling. I didn't need to feel uncomfortable or embarrassed and knew it was fine to say absolutely anything that was bothering me and get it all off my chest. I always got the support from someone who had felt the same emotions at some point of their bereavement. This stopped me feeling so out of my depth, anyone struggling is comforted and supported by other members of the community.

There was never any awkward silences or uncomfortable pauses, like the ones you get from friends who really don't know what to say to someone in your position. It was always ""me too "or "understanding hugs "then on with the conversation, leaving you feeling comforted and understood.

We were very honest and open with one another, not holding any emotion back, if we felt it we shared it by mentioning it.

There was always someone out there feeling just the same as you. There was also humour and banter too, it somehow lightened the heavy weight of your grief. It took away the dreadful loneliness too, you just log in for a chat and suddenly you are amongst friends. Like a band of faithful warriors, working together as a team to share some of the load. Coming up with suggestions and solutions for any problem you may encounter along the way as a widow and a strong independent person, struggling to carry on, but determined to succeed.

As the Macmillan and District Nurses had been so good to us, we felt we would like to give something back to them. We decided to hold a Macmillan coffee morning in our back garden. We had to time it perfectly, in between Hubby's chemo sessions, as after chemo he was always ill for several days, but then he seemed to have a really good week health wise after that. The pattern seemed to repeat itself after every session, so we could gauge when to plan it. We also needed good weather as we would all be outside, a dry preferably sunny day. We chose the first week of the school summer holidays so that my colleagues could all come.

Up went the gazebos, everyone baked cakes and brought them along to the event. Along with tombola prizes. It was an ideal chance for a lot of people to see Hubby all in the same place and in one day, saving him continual visits over a prolonged period of time. We planned that if he felt tired out by it all, he would retire up to bed for a while and rest.

Well, the weather was glorious, perhaps a little too hot, as the cakes needed a fan on them to keep cool and to prevent any icing from melting. The day was a great success, so many people came; friends, family, colleagues, neighbours, even the Mac nurse and District nurses popped in to support us and to see how we were coping.

It was such a lovely day and a really happy memory to look back on, children played and had a picnic, and adults chatted, drank coffee and ate cakes. Many people had photos taken with Hubby as keepsakes, a very poignant moment in the knowledge that this would be the last time they saw him, as he died six weeks later.

We managed to raise £500 for Macmillan cancer support that day, not a bad total for one back garden. Now Hubby has gone I plan to continue this event in his memory, perhaps every two years. Donating to such a good cause helps patients and carers get the support they need at the most dreadful time in their lives.

Lara

I came across the Macmillan Online Community Site after a few years of caring and completely by chance. I was searching for some information on the internet and one of the search results was from the site. I had a look, was impressed by how much it had to offer, joined and started reading posts and found it to be an incredible place, full of accurate, up to date information and the most amazing peer support.

How it works is you can read post on the site without having to join but if you want to reply to a post or start a new thread then you join. Joining is quick and easy. You will be anonymous as you have a user name. You are able to fill in a profile saying something about yourself and why you have joined the site which can help others get to know you or head you in the right direction but only if you feel you want to share. There is a place where you can say "hello" for the first time in the New to Site group and where I got welcoming replies and my first ever virtual hug from a wonderful woman in the Bowel Cancer Group who I learnt so much from over time.

Nick never really used the site, he didn't feel that he needed any peer support, but he did occasionally read information there on certain topics like treatment options and side effects. More often he would ask me to find something out for him next time I was on the site which I was happy to try and do.

It was a while before I started posting anything, I just read what others were talking about and found this strangely comforting. It took me a while to accept that I was a carer and belonged in the Carers Group but I also joined may other groups; the bowel cancer group, the secondary liver and lung cancer groups and the stoma group among others. Peoples' willingness to reach out a helping hand and share their experience and advice with you was quite staggering given what each and every person there was going through.

The site was just what I needed, somewhere people understood, really understood, what Nick and I were going through. Somewhere that I could give support to others as well as accept support, making me feel that at least our experience was being put to use in some small way. I felt so much less alone after joining. There was always someone online at any time of day and night.

It was my first experience of online chats and I had never realised how good it could be. Although everyone has an online name and is anonymous you developed images of people in your head and connected with people purely through the words you wrote to each other. No preconceived ideas of people, no judgement, just the power of words of help and understanding and support.

But the site is about so much more than group chats. You will find all kinds of information; videos, booklets on every aspect of cancer and each type of cancer and treatment. There is a telephone support line were you can talk to nurses, advisors and financial guides if you have financial problems or problems with your benefits.

I made some very good friends in the community, people I am still in touch with and people I have gone on to meet in the real world. I will be endlessly grateful to them and to the site for helping me through some very difficult times. I don't know how I would have done it without them.

Moods

Suzanna

As Hubby became more ill, he became understandably irritable, depressed and snappy. The medications he was on, such as steroids changed his personality completely. His moodiness was totally out of character as previously he had been a laid back, placid person, who wasn't rattled easily. I also think his frustration and lack of being able to express himself readily, left his fears and feelings showing themselves as aggression. I naturally took the brunt of his moods , as you always seem to take things out of the people you are closest to , making me prime target . I tried not to take it personally, even though I found it quite hurtful at times.

As things progressed and the pressures of it all built up, I'm ashamed to say I found myself becoming moody and snappy too. Not with Mark, but with close family and friends. I was constantly on edge, nervous and jumping at the slightest sound. I was struggling to cope with the heavy feelings of sadness and hopelessness. I was feeling useless and unable to lift his spirits despite all of my very best efforts to do so.

Calming Mark came in the shape of him sitting up all night watching TV. When I asked him why he didn't try to sleep he replied he had a series he wanted to finish watching before he died. This comment brought a massive lump to my throat, I had absolutely no answer to that. He went on to state he also enjoyed sitting up and watching dawn break ,he liked seeing daylight appear, as he didn't know how many more he would be here to see. I found this totally heart breaking.

Mark was taking cat naps all day anyway and having worked

nights for 35 years, he was still finding it difficult to turn his body clock around. Being awake all night was the norm for Hubby so I left him to it. Sometimes I would sit up with him, others I would give in to sleep as I was feeling pretty exhausted and needed to rest. If I was to be alert enough to care for him properly during the day, I would need to get some sleep at night.

For me winter months are always depressing, leaving me with a low mood. Long hours of darkness, create never ending evenings and in early widowhood I felt this even more. There is no chance of doing any gardening, everywhere is soggy, droopy and dismal. Loneliness hits hardest now and after losing Hubby, all of these feelings became magnified enormously, leaving me feeling sad and blue.

I find myself counting the days down until March arrives, the clocks go forward and I heave a sigh of relief, knowing that now my mood will lift. Spring is my favourite season, nights start to lighten up a little. Buds appear on the trees, plants and bulbs spring to life in the garden. Snowdrops, crocuses, daffodils, hyacinths and tulips, all beautiful blooms. The birds start to twitter away, the grass regrows, now I can potter about in my garden. All of these things lift my mood tremendously and the fresh air helps me sleep.

Once we hit March, all of the dreaded winter months have passed by. We now have the lovely seasons of spring, summer and autumn to look forward to, the next winter seems miles away.

Easter is coming now and I always do an Easter Egg Hunt for my Grandchildren and a few of their friends. I enjoy this every bit as much as the children do, it gives me something to look forward and to focus on. The joy on their little faces, when

Hunting Eggs is better than anything else at cheering me up and putting me in a good mood. This makes me feel that life isn't so bad after all.

Lara

Pre cancer Nick was the epitome of calm and this stayed unchanged for quite a while. In the 29 years we had been together I don't think we had had an argument. There had been "discussions" and a few, one sided, heated words but those had generally come from me. For a while he remained as level headed as ever, being rational and pragmatic about the cancer and what he was and wasn't able to do any more.

As time, and the cancer, progressed he did occasionally get a bit snappy and became self-absorbed as a very ill person can do. His treatment ruled our lives and he withdrew into himself when it was just me at home, getting cross for no real reason and confusing as well as upsetting me. He made more effort when the boys, or friends and family, were around. I suppose that I was the one person he felt he could occasionally let his guard down with or let his frustrations out with. But he had never been one for talking about his feelings much and that didn't change, I also felt he couldn't cope with my feelings. Maybe he felt guilty about what he was putting the family through and couldn't deal with that. It was the cancer, not him, that had caused all the upset and turned our lives around. Sometimes I sensed an overwhelming sadness in him but most of the time I spent second guessing how he was or what he was feeling. I did once snap back at him, saying I was doing the best I could and that I was fed up of him being so self-absorbed, retreating into himself. That it was hard for me too.

The only time he shed a tear during those five years was when our much loved dog was diagnosed with cancer and in the end was put to sleep by the vet at home as his suffering was so obvious. Mainly he was determined to carry on living, despite the cancer, within the limits of his treatment.

On the other hand I was not so calm. I used to be a worrier, the kind who will worry if there is nothing to worry about, and that continued for some time. I would worry about things going wrong during surgery and treatment, about side effects, about how our sons were coping and Nick was really feeling, about having all the necessary medications in the house and the right food in the fridge. Was the house clean enough, would friends with a cough or a cold know to stay away, would I cope. The worries I had and the stress they caused were exacerbated by some other big family problems that occurred at the same time and my moods swung from desperation and depression to anger and determination.

I have always been a coper told myself that if I was coping, without the need for any help, then I was doing alright. Of course this wasn't the best way to be and eventually I had to admit that I wasn't actually coping at all and felt that I was letting everyone down by not being able to do everything and hold everything together anymore. But, rather than reach out and ask for the help and support I needed I just decided, subconsciously, to shut off any feeling and just get on with the practical things. Those I could deal with.

If Nick had a problem that he needed help with I focused on that problem, rather than the whole picture. Sometimes he got big clots of blood and phlegm from his chest that he found hard to cough up. Occasionally he would struggle so much he had a panic attack and would start choking. I would then have to put my hand to the very back of his throat and pull the clot out for him. I'd dress the open wound on his leg and try to stem the flow of blood from his stoma while we got him to hospital so that they could cauterise it. I stayed calm as they told us the cancer had gone to his brain and when the cancer became more aggressive.

Looking back I think in order to help Nick live I merely existed, especially during the later years. I loved him and cared for him but I largely stopped caring for and about myself. I would still worry about our boys and do my best for them but looking back I feel I let them down.

There was the odd occasion when I would cry, but it was rare and usually very late at night when everyone had gone to bed. It was as though I was full of unshed tears and had to leak a few to stop me overflowing.

Some time after Nick's death I was still not feeling anything, to a point where our sons were commenting on it. It wasn't just that I couldn't express my feelings, I actually felt like I couldn't feel. Help from a very patient counsellor has meant I can begin to feel again.

Fears and Worries

Suzanna

It's hard to imagine how someone who has been a constant presence in your life for so many years, could suddenly not physically be there anymore. It's even harder to imagine never seeing them again for the rest of your life. It's seems surreal and very hard to process. Just thinking about it would have my stomach gambolling over and over. This was my life partner, what life would I have without him and how would our boys cope with the loss of their father?

So, I tried not to think about it at all and kept my fears and worries hidden, by burying them deep into the back of my mind and then just concentrating on blocking them right out. I mastered the art and in the main, it worked well for me. I managed to keep myself very busy, allowing no time for dark thoughts to enter my head and to always be occupied with other matters.

Deep down I knew I was kidding myself and eventually I would be forced to face my worst fears. Hubby and I were both scared, but hid the fact from each other, as best we could. A sort of survival tactic I think. Almost as if we didn't say it, it wasn't happening.

There were things that needed sorting out, Mark's wishes, financial affairs, jobs around the house, to mention just a few. But I was worried about touching on the subjects, as he was not ready to discuss these things and I would have felt awful for asking him to do so. Almost as if I had written him off before his time.

If it had been me, I would have wanted my affairs in order and planned ahead. In fact I would have made my wishes crystal clear and constantly drummed them home to my family. I will do just that when my time comes. But we are all different and cope in different ways. I'm a very methodical person, Mark wanted to wait, it was his choice and I had to honour that.

In the end a lot of it was allowed to slide until it was way too late to do anything about it. And sadly some things were not arranged as they could have been leaving me with a lot more things to sort out, things that could have been seen to while he was alive. But I understood why he couldn't face them. I was heavily weighed down with the paper work and it all became too much for me to cope with on my own so I used a solicitor.

Lara

I am very aware that in some aspects we were more fortunate than other families dealing with terminal cancer. We had no financial worries as Nick was still receiving a percentage of his salary, we could afford to stay in our home and pay our bills. I remember feeling such sadness for a carer, on an on line forum, who had to move while her husband was desperately ill as they could no longer afford the home they had. I can't imagine how traumatic that must have been. We are also a tight knit family and I am aware neither is that always the case.

But I still had fears and worries. I worried about being able to care for Nick and look after him to the level he needed caring for sometimes wondering if I was doing a good enough job. I worried about the children and whether I was giving them enough support. I was terrified of the life without him that I knew was coming. I had fears around his treatment, what side effects he may have, whether he would wake up from surgery. Would I be able to hold him as he died? What if I wasn't there when he died and he was alone?

The hardest thing about these fears and worries was that I often had no one to talk to about them. Nick was so focussed on his treatment and getting to his next landmark that he often didn't seem to have the capacity to listen to my fears and when he did I worried about burdening him more than he was already burdened. My closest sibling had a serious health issue of her own and it felt wrong to off load on her. I seemed to still spend more time listening to friends and comforting them than the other way around. I imagine it could be painful listening and many people can't deal with that. I didn't want my children to worry about me as well as their dad.

When I was seeing a counsellor at least I had 50 minutes a week to let go and share how I really felt inside but that was limited to 12 weeks and the time didn't necessarily tie in with when I needed to talk. There was the online forum but I found it hard to share my innermost feelings there as some carers were able to.

My release was my daily walks when I could escape the real world for a while. I put in my ear phones, turned up the music and walked, fast or slow as my mood took me, with the dog running in circles around me exploring the smells of the woods. My headspace time which was invaluable to me.

The Loving Relationship

Suzanna

Mark was never very demonstrative with his feelings of love at the best of times. I always went to him for hugs and he always obliged by hugging me back. I just wish he had come to me first sometimes and thrown his arms around me spontaneously.

I told him I loved him daily and he always replied "I love you too". But he never said it first. I knew full well he loved me and never at any time doubted it. It was just he struggled to show his feelings and was basically a very shy and private man.

He was always there for me and would do anything for me. But he would never make a display of his love. He didn't like to draw attention to himself, and would far rather just blend into the background. He always sent me lovely cards and flowers for Birthdays and Anniversaries, but he wasn't really a romantic type and definitely not a spur of the moment man in any way. Always subdued and low key.

When he was very ill in hospital with pulmonary embolisms and a big chance he may not pull through, our Macmillan Nurse sat with us and encouraged us to talk about love and death. So should the worst happen, nothing would be left unsaid? A sort of open and honest goodbye talk, in case it was necessary. She was trying to make sure we put everything in order, leaving no regrets or feelings of words unsaid left behind.

The "love you" bit was easy, we did that daily. But talking of his death was way too hard and we avoided the subject, almost denying it could ever happen to us. But it could and it would.

Lara

Cancer took its toll on more than just Nick's body, it took a toll on our relationship. If you are caring for your spouse or partner day in day out over several years the emotions can be hard to bear at times and so, for me and I think for him as well, there was a tendency to switch them off and just get on with the jobs in hand. For me as a carer and for him as a terminally ill person unwilling to let go of life easily. Cancer can rob you of your physical relationship, it did us, and if you shy away from the emotional relationship that doesn't leave you with much. Or does it?

We loved each other, we didn't tell each other every day but we knew, and we were great friends. No-one else would care for Nick in the way I was prepared to, anyway he didn't want them to and I wouldn't let them. We knew each other so well that there were things we didn't need to verbalise, we just "knew".

Talking about emotions happened rarely and if it did it was me talking. I know it was painful for him. In a letter he left me to read after he was dead he apologised for distancing himself from me and said he hoped I knew it was a coping strategy nothing else. I think I did know but it hadn't been easy. Giving him hugs had become so difficult because of his neuropathy, his scar tissue, his stoma. I couldn't stroke his hair or hold his hand easily as the neuropathy made that too painful. There were times I lay in bed at night full of anger that my husband couldn't hold me in his arms any more as I went to sleep and I remember reaching out a foot to touch his leg just to feel some physical contact with the man I loved. There were days I felt rejected and unloved but of course it was just the cancer to blame and how ill my poor love was. This was when "find pleasure in the simple things in life" became a phrase of ours. Watching a TV programme together, sitting in the garden and watching the birds and insects, walking with the dog when he was able, little food treats, the family evenings.

When Nick was getting nearer to death we were told to say everything we needed, or wanted, to each other but he still wouldn't talk. He said he didn't feel like he had anything unsaid to say. No regrets, no upset. We knew what we meant to each other and he couldn't think about what my life would be like without him as he wouldn't be there. He said I'd be okay, that was all. I don't think he could deal with any discussion. We did discuss his funeral in very broad terms; simple, no fuss, a celebration not a mourning, I would get it right. Discussion over.

Family and Friends

Suzanna

It was very kind how family and friends tried to help and support us but on occasion it could be too many people too often. Sometimes it could be an extra strain to deal with anyone other than Mark, there just wasn't the time or energy. Here are some thoughts for anyone who wants to help someone in the same situation we were in.

When phoning to enquire how the patient is doing, take time to ask how the carer is coping too. Often a complete conversation is held concerning the patient, but people rarely think to ask after the carer. They will be having a tough time and maybe overwhelmed by the enormity of it all too. If they are struggling, a few words of support and understanding can go a long way and be appreciated. When visiting a gentle hand squeeze or a hug can show you are thinking of them and want to help out. Try not to make visits too long, the patient will tire easily and the carer will be under enormous pressure, a sympathetic visitor will sense when it's time to leave.

Once you have asked how they both are, listen to the answers, I mean really listen, as many clues of how they are both doing can be given away here. A good listener will be able to read between the lines and pick up on the unspoken fears, feelings and needs behind the" we are fine" statement that we all use .

Offer to help out, but if your help is refused at this point, don't take it as a rebuff or an insult in any way. It may be that they just need time and space together alone, to deal with their own emotions. Remember that this is about them and all that they are having to deal and come to terms with. Give them all the privacy they need to adjust to this new life that has been thrown at them so unexpectedly and wholly unwantedly.

Just be ready and waiting in the wings, offer your support at regular intervals, don't withdraw your support or get offended by a refusal. Keep offering and be prepared to step in when you are needed. That is what families and friends do for each other at such times, pull together and help whichever way you can .Sometimes helping can be in the shape of standing back and waiting for just the right time to come forward. Knowing that you were there by their sides when they really needed you, One day your kindness will be returned and you will receive the thanks you deserve just for being around at an awful time for everyone concerned.

If you do get a chat with the patient try to keep it upbeat, not all doom and gloom or depressing, some news, sport, the weather anything they can relate to. A laugh and a joke is still possible and can lift the patient's mood. Ask them if there is anything they want you to do for them, or if they want to talk about how they feel or offload their worries to a listening ear. Sometimes they are ready to share a problem or a job that needs doing and are glad you asked. Maybe they can tell you things they don't want to burden their partner with, maybe you can help, and these kind offers go a long way towards putting the patient's mind at rest. Goodness knows what goes through the mind of someone with a terminal prognosis, it must be very scary for them. You will then be able to rest assured that you did everything you possibly could for them both to ease the pressure of a dreadful situation.

Lara

Many carers I have spoken to said that when you have a crisis in your life you find out who your true friends are and I understand how they felt. I certainly found out a lot more about our friends and family members and was very surprised by some peoples' reaction to our situation both in a positive and less positive way.

There were wonderful people who truly wanted to help and just instinctively knew how they could do that. They would take the dogs out for a walk, or do some shopping for us when we hadn't had time as Nick was in hospital. There was a friend who visited regularly and spent time with Nick giving him a few hours of normality and me a few hours to go off and get some jobs done or have a sleep. Friends would come at short notice, bringing lunch with them, and sit at the table with us and laugh and joke and catch up. Before Nick was ill I used to visit my friend with cancer and would take my friend to an appointment to give her partner a break or just sit and chat with her or watch a film or take her for a drive if she felt like it, to give her partner a bit of time to himself. I would try to cut the grass or do some house chores while she slept, any little job that I could see needed doing. It gave me something to do and was one less thing for an already drained carer to do later on.

The people who were the greatest support to us weren't necessarily those we expected to be and kindness came from so many places. There was our dog walker/ sitter (who we used on days spent at hospital) who would often turn up and say they were walking a dog in the area and wanted to take ours with it. Our hairdresser who sent so many cards, some funny, some caring, with the most wonderful messages, because she wanted us to know she was always thinking of us. Our neighbour was always ready with a hug and a cup of tea or a glass of wine when I was in need and there was the friend who would ask me how I was, listen to my generic reply, then asked the right questions to find out how I really was and listen again.

There are also those who, I am sure, wanted to help us but maybe just didn't know how to. Maybe they didn't want to get dragged into a situation they couldn't cope with. Maybe they thought I really was coping on my own or maybe they were waiting for me to ask for help.

Some people, including family members, expected us to carry on in the same way we always had and some who vanished altogether. A few who vanished have tried to come back into my life now and I am trying to let them in. They will have had their reasons for choosing to leave us behind.
Nick's family, his parents and his brothers, were very absent during those 5 years. We got newspaper articles in the post from his mother, about miracle cures and the evils of traditional treatment. Letters would arrive saying he could be cured by stopping eating and living on freshly juiced vegetables (well, that would have been an explosive disaster with his stoma bag...) and that he didn't need radiotherapy plus many, many others. But she didn't visit, she didn't spend quality time with her son and when we were able to visit their house they acted as if Nick was fit and healthy, cancer and treatment wasn't mentioned. I don't know what it was, head in the sand, denial, or whether they really believed the articles they sent us. All I know was that his parents were absent, they didn't visit our house, hospital, the hospice or say goodbye to him.

His brothers were equally absent offering and giving little or no support. This made me sad and angry for Nick. He had always been there to help and support his brothers and now he was the one in need there was nothing. One brother did say to me that I should feel free to ask for help if I needed it and he would feel free to say no if it wasn't convenient. Well, what do you say to that! But Nick was as calm as ever and said that if they couldn't deal with the situation then that was sad but just the way it was.

My family is small but close and were mainly a great support, dropping everything to come and hold the fort at home if we needed them to, but again there were those who just stayed away. That hurt. A lot.

I think no-one can understand what it is like living with an incurable disease, or with a loved one who has one, unless they have been unfortunate to have experienced it first-hand I believe, and we weren't about to share all the details of what Nick went through with everyone. We were usually positive, often upbeat, and Nick put on a very "normal" face to the outside world. We liked to laugh and enjoy the simple things in life still, it was certainly not all doom and gloom in our house.   But underneath life was often challenging. We were permanently exhausted and always had interrupted nights as Nick's stoma bag needed emptying, often several times a night or he was in pain and couldn't get comfortable or he had an appointment coming up that was on our minds. As the years passed we were more tired and the day to day tasks became a struggle to keep on top of. My stress and anxiety didn't help.

There were things I would have liked to say to those people who stayed away or didn't know what to do. At the time I didn't have the energy or time to deal with it or even know what I would say but hindsight is a wonderful thing.

I'd want them to understand that it's okay not to know what to say or do. They could just have said "I don't know what to say". It would have been better than saying nothing at all.

Just because we were going through difficult times didn't mean that by visiting us or supporting us they'd be dragged down in anyway. Supporting a friend of mine through cancer was incredibly rewarding, an honour, and there were many new good memories made. Our home was not a depressing place to visit. We liked to laugh and chat and live. We were very unlikely to burst out crying or unburden ourselves on anyone, we enjoyed the normality of good time spent with family and friends.

Some people needed to understand we couldn't carry on as before. We may not be able to, or want to, cook for visitors, or have them stay as long as they wanted. As time went on if people wanted to visit Nick we would fit them in but they needed to phone to check it was convenient and that Nick and I were up to them coming. If we said a short visit then there was a reason for that, what mattered was Nick and how he was.

We may not have got to the shops and there may not be biscuits to offer or even tea sometimes and if they were there we may not remember to offer them. We hoped people would expect nothing and be happy to have whatever we could offer that day, then we wouldn't feel guilty or bad for being poor hosts. For many families dealing with cancer their income has been impacted. Something else for visitors to bear in mind.

The best kind of help was when people gave us the support and practical help we wanted and needed not what they thought we needed.

Articles on "miracle cures" were not appreciated. Anyone who knew us should have known that we'd have done so much research on every possible treatment option and come to our own informed opinions rather than seeing a random article and sending it on to us without any understanding of Nick's cancer.

Cancer is unpredictable and comparing Nick's cancer to a friend's sister's cancer or a work colleagues cancer and thinking you understand is not necessarily helpful. Everyone's illness is unique to them and how their body handles it and progression can be unpredictable. Treatment that works for one person may not work for another.

There are different types of support that can be given; practical, social and emotional. If someone couldn't help with one then maybe they could help with another. Honestly, it feels good to help, any you can give will be appreciated so much and we would never have expected or asked too much of anyone.

Last Holiday

Suzanna and Mark

When Mark had his good weeks in between chemo we tried to make the most of his 'well ' days. We pre-planned days out, visitors coming and filled the days as happily as we could, given the circumstances. He desperately wanted to see the sea one last time, so I mentioned this in passing to our community Macmillan Nurse. She felt that, yes, he was well enough to travel at the time and saw no reason why we couldn't have a mini break away.

There is a Hotel in Bournemouth called The Grove that caters especially for cancer patients and those with life threatening illnesses. This was to be the perfect Hotel, in the perfect location as Bournemouth is known for its warm air and is a stunning year round resort. The Grove is owned and operated by Macmillan Caring Locally. Their aim is to support patients as well as their carers and family members. The Hotel has a qualified Nurse on call 24 hours a day in case of an emergency, but no hands on nursing is available. It is non - profit making, but extends its support by offering a welcome retreat for those who need and deserve it.

Our Community Macmillan Nurse kindly did all the necessary paperwork for us , declaring Mark's illness and stating she felt he was well enough to travel , then she booked us a short break there. His twin sister and her husband offered to drive us down there and bring us back. This was a massive factor to us being able to go, we would never have managed to get there and back without their support.

The weather was absolutely glorious, we couldn't have picked a better week. A very warm welcome awaited us and we were shown to our beautiful and spacious room , with facilities , such as an emergency call button in the bedroom and an emergency pull cord in the bathroom , heated towel rails , a set of towels and toiletries and a direct dial telephone in every room . So if you needed help quickly you could easily raise the alarm. There were lifts to every floor and a level entrance to the hotel, giving easy wheelchair access. They also had a number of mobility scooters and wheelchairs for guests to use .They had lovely grounds with a summer house to relax in and both sunny and shaded areas and a large conservatory to look onto the grounds from. They also had a large lounge and a drinks bar room.

On the beach they owned a beach hut for guest use.   We had a fabulous time there, nothing was too much trouble for the staff during our stay. The food was delicious and nutritious, we enjoyed the company of other guests and were greeted at Breakfast daily by the Manager and Nurses, all checking if we were ok and enjoying our stay, or needing anything they could provide for us.

We managed to go on all the day trips, they had their own mini bus and we were chauffeur driven around, people even took time to stop and wave when they saw the Macmillan sign on the bus, doormen tipped their hats as we drove past, it was touching and heart-warming .We saw some beautiful sights that week, we even managed a boat trip. Despite Hubby struggling to breath at times and needing his oxygen, he kept up incredibly well and thoroughly enjoyed it, an afternoon nap refreshed him for supper and gave me a little break to read and relax.

On the last evening there was a firework display from the

beach, but as the guests were sick people we couldn't go down there.

We had made some friends who had a corner room on the top floor and they invited us up for drinks, with the hope we may see a few fireworks from their room. Bless them. Well we had a panoramic view up there and I believe we saw nearly all of the fireworks, which Hubby enjoyed immensely. They were such kind and sharing people to invite us up there as it was their anniversary and they shared their champagne with us.

I look back on that precious time together fondly, as Hubby died very shortly after our break, about a month later he was gone, making that last Holiday incredibly special and leaving me both treasured memories and pictures to look back on when I feel sad.

Last Chance

Suzanna

Mark dragged himself to his last clinic appointment with sheer grit and determination, not wanting to give in. I had rung into our Macmillan Nurses at the Hospital, to ask if one of them could kindly come into the appointment to support us through it. We already knew it was the worst news possible and would be distressing. Although late in the day and after their normal hours, one of our lovely nurses offered to stay behind and give us support. That single act of kindness, will remain with me always. Their wonderful caring natures are the reason I will always support Macmillan Nurses.

He tried so hard to 'look' well enough for more treatment. Stepping out of his wheelchair and taking off his oxygen mask before entering the Oncologist's room. My wonderful brave Man was not giving in without one hell of a fight and I loved him for that. So brave, strong and determined. Both the Oncologist and the Nurse looked visibly moved by his courage and so was I!

The Oncologist said there would be no more IV chemo sessions, he really wasn't strong enough, it could even kill him outright. But as he was still fighting, he would offer him a course of Tarceva tablets as a last ditch attempt, although a slim one, that it may help. Hubby was so grateful and readily accepted the offer, he was prepared to do or take anything, to prolong his life. He was going to fight on for as long as he possibly could.

The Macmillan Nurse sat beside me, holding my hand throughout the appointment. Silent tears ran down my cheeks continually, whilst we were in the room. But I didn't make a sound, not a squeak , Hubby couldn't see me as I was sat behind him and I swallowed down the enormous loud sobs that were threatening to escape from deep within me. I also stifled the urge to scream, like a howling banshee, I needed to stay strong for Hubby.

The Oncologist looked at me, full of pity, as we left the room he squeezed my arm gently, but knowingly and supportively. The Macmillan Nurse took us into another room to discuss the new treatment and its side effects. Then as we left for home she gave me a massive hug.

Hubby was determined that these new tablets would work for him and he would see an improvement soon. Unfortunately this was not the case, the tablets did nothing to help. In fact, with the side effects, they only made things worse. Our Community Mac Nurse suggested he just come off them, explaining that they were now taking away what little quality of life he had left. Hubby was having none of it. He was convinced they would 'kick in ' soon. But his health just took a nose dive and went down and down.

He became weaker daily, gasping for breath, even with oxygen. He then started having panic attacks, when he couldn't breathe properly, more angina attacks and started coughing up blood, it was awful. I helped him by calming him through the panic and slowing his breathing down. But we now needed more support and we were referred to our local Hospice for their input.

Counselling

Suzanna

Being Mark's carer was the most important job I had ever undertaken. But sometimes it was also the most difficult, with him being so desperately ill, I often felt terribly sad and lonely. It started to take its toll on me emotionally and I struggled to stay on top of it all. I had so many things running through my head, so how must he have felt? I wondered if counselling may help us to handle some of the many issues we were now facing. I felt I needed it, but Mark refused it, he was a very private person, a closed book.

I spoke to my Mac Nurse about how I was feeling and if any counselling was available. She said they offered it there at the hospital for cancer patients and their families. She was going to refer me, when suddenly the reality of it made me backtrack (nerves). I said I wasn't completely sure if I wanted it yet but she said now you have spoken to me I need to refer you on, it becomes my duty.

I was put on the waiting list and I received a letter asking me to opt in, if I still wanted counselling and they would contact me as soon as an appointment became available. I waited a while, then received an appointment in the post.

Counselling turned out to be the best thing I ever did. If the patient has a terminal diagnosis you are deprived of any hope of a future together. This in itself is a massive issue to come to terms with, as hope is something to cling onto, it keeps you going throughout treatment. Once that is taken away from you, you are left with a heavy feeling of impending doom, weighed down with sorrow, how do you carry on?

Counselling commenced in a small room at the hospital, My Counsellor was a lovely, gently spoken man. The first session was really an introduction to each other, to see if he felt I needed counselling and if we could feel comfortable enough to work together. If you don't feel comfortable, you will never open up about your fears, feelings and all of the questions on your mind that are bothering you. It's essential to have a good rapport with each other, to have quality, and productive sessions. I liked him immediately, he was patient, kind, and he also had a lovely soothing Irish lilt. I was very nervous, but we filled the one hour slot by doing a family tree. This opened up a point of conversation and created some ground work. It also made the time pass quickly. At the end of the session he asked if I thought I would benefit from some counselling and did I feel I could talk to him. I said yes definitely, hence my counselling began.

We talked about anything and everything, no holds barred. Everything I said was totally confidential, enabling me to get all of my worries off my chest, with the knowledge that it would never hurt anyone's feelings, or get repeated. After some sessions I felt better, but after others, I felt much worse. I believe this to be the norm, as you are bringing thoughts and feelings that may have been deeply buried, up to the surface. Feelings, that once exposed, have to be faced and dealt with. But it's all part of the healing process, there were inevitably tears, occasionally anxiety attacks and sometimes humour." Its ok to laugh you know "he kindly said, when I was feeling guilty for seeing the funny side of things. But humour keeps you going, lightens the load.

We tried to book sessions on the days Mark had chemo, as we were at the Hospital anyway, so I knew he wasn't alone. I always sat with him for his chemo sessions, so an hour of counselling allowed him a little nap and me a breather. It worked well and for a while became routine. I could relax as I knew he had Nurses around him, if he needed them , but he was always ok when I returned, generally snoozing or sipping tea .

There was a spell when he was an inpatient, but I still managed counselling around visiting. As I got to know my counsellor, I didn't feel quite so nervous. At times I talked continuously and joked about him needing to lie down in a darkened room when I left. I kept saying I would bring him ear plugs next time, then he could just nod his head at regular intervals, not hearing a word I am saying , he took it all in good part.

On a serious note, it was helping me enormously,   I no longer felt embarrassed if I cried, I think it was because he didn't react other than to hand me tissues. He taught me relaxation techniques for when I was anxious and later a way to handle the awful flashbacks from when Hubby died. I really feel counselling got me through the worst ordeal of my life. He never judged me just sat quietly listening and never reacting.

I saw him for a few months before Mark died, then continued to see him until 12 months after his death. He helped me to come to terms with a massive loss. Sometimes I cried all the way there on the bus, just the thought of counselling could set me off. But slowly I got over that stage and felt more in control. When we felt we had discussed everything possible and I had reached a point when I felt more able to cope, we had a couple of wind down sessions and then counselling concluded. I will always remember my counsellor with fondness and gratitude, for his kindness, patience, his gentle way and his wonderful techniques. He gave me a massive amount of support at a very sad and difficult time.

What have I gained from counselling?

- I could cry freely there, without feeling embarrassed.
- I have learnt a breathing technique, for when I'm anxious.
- I was taught how to deal with dreadful flashbacks.
- I faced my grief, together with the enormity and complexity of it.
- I have learnt how to take care of myself now.
- I learnt that talking about my loss, although painful, does help.
- I'm learning to look to the future, not the past.
- I'm learning how to solve my own problems independently.
- I'm feeling a much stronger person, thanks to counselling.
- I can now stand on my own two feet and cope alone.

Could counselling help you?

- Only you will know if you are ready for counselling, regardless of which stage of the journey you are at.
- Find a counsellor that you are comfortable with and can open up to.
- Be ready for some soul searching questions, to digging down deep into your fears and facing them head on.
- Take little steps into the future at a pace that you are ready for and can cope with.
- Be prepared to go on a waiting list, counselling is very much sought after and very busy.
- Stick with it even if you feel worse before you feel better.
- It should be a rewarding experience in the long run.

Lara

I never thought of myself as someone who would turn to counselling. Talking about my feelings and the situation we were in wasn't something that came naturally and I was a "coper", I dealt with what was thrown at me. Or I thought I did.

But one day I found myself in the GP surgery telling my doctor that I was struggling and thought I needed some help. It was after a particularly bad period. Nick was having a tough time with treatment, my sister was having a lot of treatment for her breast cancer and I had just had a big cancer scare myself. In fact I had been told I had cancer and when the results of the biopsy came back clear the clinic didn't trust them and they took 10 more biopsies. How was I going to care for Nick, my sons and my parents if I was undergoing treatment as well as him? The whole thing took about 6 weeks to get the all clear.

My doctor got me to sit in his room and fill out several self-assessment forms and then said he thought I was "under reporting" how I felt and he would put me forward for some counselling as he thought it could help me. I had said I didn't want medication so this was the option left and I took it. Within a few weeks I had had a telephone assessment, a face to face assessment and I was told that they thought I would benefit most from one to one rather than group counselling and I would be contacted when a place became available. I was relieved and desperate to get started as I knew that I was struggling to keep on top of things.

After 4 months I still hadn't heard anything. When you are struggling and depressed it is hard to push for anything but I got on the phone to ask how much longer it would be. I was told up to a month. After nearly 6 months and still not hearing I felt at breaking point, like I was about to boil over. It took me several days but eventually I managed to pick up the phone again to ask how much longer. This time I was told at least one month maybe two. I explained how long I had been waiting and was told that was the waiting list and she was sorry but there was nothing she could do. Well, that was the point I boiled over. I was sobbing so much I couldn't talk or at least what I was saying couldn't be heard and in the end I just apologised and said good bye and hung up. I had been desperate when I went to the GP, I wouldn't have gone otherwise. To make people who are desperate for help wait and wait felt cruel although I understood what pressure the service was under.

Two days later I received a phone call. My case had been reviewed and they could offer me a different type of counselling starting in two weeks if I was happy to accept that. I really didn't know there were different types of counselling. I felt a mixture of relief to have a date to see someone and guilt at feeling I had somehow skipped the queue.

The counsellor soon realised that I wasn't in a position of control in my life. The things I had to deal with weren't choices or things that could be solved, they were what they were. So we spent the sessions with me having some time and space to talk and feel with him listening and teaching me some strategies and techniques that could help me sleep or cope a little better.

Talking helped, it helped even more when I was talking to someone who you are not trying to protect from the full force of the emotions inside you. I didn't need to spare his feelings or worry about whether he could cope with what he was hearing and it did me good. At least it did me good eventually, there were days when I didn't want to go and open up all the pain and in the early days I often left feeling exhausted and worse than when I had arrived but it got better, easier. When it got to my last session I felt a wave of panic. What would I do without that window each week but that was the way the system worked. He said he would recommend me for more counselling but I couldn't bear the thought of another lengthy wait.

Since Nick died I have been having some more counselling and this time it is more than talking, it is helping me to find a way forward to a life I didn't want and didn't expect but which I now have. And again it is helping but this time in a more useful and constructive way. It can still be tough and painful some weeks but I will keep going until I feel ready to strike out on my own.

When The Cancer is Incurable

Suzanna

Mark being given an incurable cancer diagnosis emotionally equated to being hit with a sledge hammer full pelt. It was one hell of a blow, the enormity of it all took some time to fully sink in and process, even longer to accept. Your mind races over every possibility and then some. Are they sure? How long has he got? How could that time be prolonged? What do we do and who will we turn to now? The questions are a whirlpool in your head, many of them unanswerable, as medics can only give a rough estimate, a ' guesstimate ', of any time scales involved until the last stage of the disease. It's not an exact science and can vary widely from one person to the next.

To prolong life with treatment has its own risks with possibilities of blood clots, heart attack, life threatening infections, reactions and horrific side effects. We had to weigh up the pros and cons and decide what was right in our individual case. Was it best to take any treatment possible and grab every extra minute of life on offer, despite the risks? Or should we just take the "watch and wait" path, knowing the cancer could spread rapidly? The decision was massive.

For Mark it was always the treatment route. But for me? Well, I just didn't want to lose him and would stand by him in any and every choice he took. It's awful having to watch your loved one go through rounds of gruelling treatment and its dreadful side effects. But it was how we chose to handle it, together as a couple and as part of a united family team.

We faced it head on, rolled our sleeves up ready for a fight, all be it a losing one, we would fight none the less.
When the diagnosis of incurable cancer has a very poor prognosis, as in our case where the estimated life expectancy was approximately 3 months without treatment and 6 months with it, we received palliative care from a network of people. A palliative care team may include an oncologist, specialist nurse, your GP, district nurses and community Macmillan nurses. A local hospice can also provide support. A family should never feel unsupported or left to cope alone and we weren't.

Lara

The survival rates for many types of cancer are improving and the length of time a person can live with incurable cancer is growing. But, barring any sudden miracle treatment, incurable will mean just that.

As treatments improve there has developed a clear distinction between an incurable and a terminal illness. Nick lived with the knowledge that he had incurable cancer for 5 years. For much of that time it was incurable but treatable; there was some comfort in that. He decided that he could sit around and wait to die or he could carry on living as full and as positive a life as he could. He chose the latter.

Nick lived for five years with cancer, well, five years when we knew he had the disease, probably at least two more years before diagnosis. Treatment started relatively quickly and continued, mainly on but occasionally off, until less than 2 weeks before he died. We quickly learnt to make the most of the days when he was feeling well and not to push things when he was feeling grotty. For the first year working gave him routine, structure and normality which I think he needed very much at that time. For the rest of the family it was a period of adjustment. Getting used to having him at home all the time, as he had previously been away most of each week, and getting used to the new life that came with treatment and uncertainty.

He didn't want to be treated like an invalid or a patient, he simply wanted to carry on being who he had always been and keep his independence as far as he could for as long as he could.

He got to see our sons reach big milestones in their lives and kept setting himself new targets. Seeing one son finish school and move to university, the other finish university, knowing they both had good jobs to go to and that they were making their own lives. He was so proud of all they managed to achieve and wanted to be part of it.

He carried on living so I carried on helping him live. It wasn't always easy. I hated seeing what he was having to deal with but then I was so thankful that he was still around to deal with it. I think on some level I was holding my breath waiting to be told that was it, no more treatment, time was limited but in the end that was Nick's choice not the doctors'.

We started appreciating the simple things in life, a walk by the river, a coffee, lunch with friends, doing the crossword together, watching a TV programme from episode one to the final episode, pottering around the garden and in the potting shed, listening to the boys and their friends who often filled the house with laughter and laughing with them.

Of course things got harder. Nick became more ill, more limited in what he could do, needing 24hour oxygen, and a wheelchair. But he carried on trying to live within the confines the disease created for him.

I think that Nick and I were pretty realistic about his diagnosis but there were those who weren't. As he continued to beat the odds some family and friends seemed to think that he was also going to beat the disease. I would hope for good scan results, something that showed the treatment was worthwhile and I admit that for a while, especially following good results, I hoped for and dreamt of a miracle. A cure for the incurable. But for me hope proved to be totally exhausting and unhelpful. Not the hoping for more time, good time, that Nick could enjoy, that went on, but hoping for a miracle. That hope could twist me up in knots and make me forget to breathe properly, take over my mind for a while and then on the occasions results weren't so good the crash was hard and painful.

Over time what worked better for me was acceptance. Nick would live with cancer for as long as he lived but the cancer would kill him, I didn't dwell on the fact but I didn't deny it either. There was nothing I could do that would affect the results of scans so I tried very hard to accept that they would be what they would be and we would deal with it. Planning something and accepting we may have to cancel at the last minute was less trying than planning and hoping that all would be okay on the day.

When Nick was first referred to the palliative care team he was very anti the idea. To him palliative meant the nearing of the end of his life but he grew to realise that it means so much more than this and the care he received helped him stay mobile and active. As end of life approached his biggest concerns were to have as little pain as possible and to be as calm as possible. One place that truly understood this and palliative care in general was the hospice. We became involved with them several months before Nick died and the help and support we received was outstanding. The nurse who used to visit the house was wonderful and full of hints and tips to help with the pain, the cough, and the breathlessness. His pain control was constantly reviewed and amended as necessary. For the first time he was given meds to help with the panic attacks and just knowing they were there if he needed them was a comfort and a support to him.

I think Nick's final goal was to see our younger son through his final exams at University. He tried so hard but the final type of chemo he had been put on caused unbearable side effects and so he took the very brave decision to end treatment. His oncologist talked this through with him and after suggesting some alternatives, which Nick rejected, he accepted his decision. He said that, without treatment, Nick was likely to live for 2 to 3 months.

It was the toughest thing since telling them he had incurable cancer to tell the boys of his decision but they were so brave. They knew how hard things had become for him, they accepted his choice. I also accepted it but hadn't done so easily. I think I had been using his goals as my crutch, telling myself he would still be here for each landmark he set. In reality it took me some days to accept the fact that he couldn't, wouldn't, carry on living much longer. I was so scared. So, so scared of facing a life without him.

The day he made the decision not only did he have unbearable ulceration of mouth and throat that meant he could hardly drink let alone eat, he was also found to have an infection, and so the decision was made that he would go into hospital to be treated for that and then move to the local hospice for pain relief and some respite. We accepted this as we hoped to spend some time together when someone else was doing all the nursing side of caring and looking after him and he and I could be husband and wife again rather than patient and carer. The plan was he would then come home, with a proper care plan in place, until the end when he would return to the hospice to die.

The End stages of Life.

Suzanna

By now Hubby's oxygen saturation level was down to 80%, even when sitting still and using oxygen. Any slight movement and he turned grey. He was literally gasping for breath and struggling to do so. His health had deteriorated drastically.

One morning, our Community Macmillan Nurse visited us unannounced. She was shortly followed by a Lead District Nurse. This in itself was very unusual, as they had never visited us unannounced or on the same day before. They usually told us when they were coming and also left messages for each other in Mark's care plan folder, arranging visits around each other to save resources. So seeing them arrive together unsettled us, as today it appeared they had pre-arranged to meet each other at our house.

They both had a serious expression on their faces and said they needed to speak to us both .They said Hubby was now very ill and no plans had been made for his end of life care. Also a DNR form needed to be signed by him and our GP and placed into his records. This meant that he would not be resuscitated should he have a heart attack, which was very upsetting to hear. But we understood why these things now needed planning and putting into action. Mark appeared to be blocking it out by not responding in any way to the conversation but he did sign the form. I was in tears and they tried to comfort us by gently explaining it was time to make decisions and they would be there to support us through whatever we decided to do. Hubby's records were taken away to update and to add a DNR form and returned later that day.

Our Community Macmillan Nurse rang his Oncologist, to confirm he was coming to the end of his life. No time scales were given, but it wouldn't be long. She decided now was the time to speak to our sons. As they all work, she kindly offered an early morning meet at our house. Our Sons and their partners arrived first, then our Macmillan Nurse appeared, bringing a trainee Macmillan Nurse along with her.

She gently explained that their Dad didn't have long left to live. It was a very emotional time, many tears were shed that morning, and it was heart breaking to watch. I stayed strong, comforting my Sons and partners one by one. I had already been given this news, but now it was time to tell them, it was their Dad and they had a right and needed to know. Then they left us to discuss Hubby's wishes about where he wanted to die. As a family we sat down and debated the pros and cons of Home / Hospice / Hospital and I took notes of all of our comments as a guide to show how we felt. It was the hardest thing that we, as a family had ever had to face, but face it we must.

When the District Nurse came the next day I showed her our check list and she said it was a really good idea, an open and honest list of everyone's thoughts. She asked if she could take a copy to use for training purposes. I was happy for her to have one, as I feel that anything that could possibly help others had to be a good thing.

A lady from the Hospice came to visit us at home shortly after, sent by the Mac Nurse, to talk to us and to offer Hubby a bed there. But Hubby was still insisting he was nowhere near ready to go in yet, maybe later on he would consider it. Despite the fact that, Unknown to us he only had six days left to live! So she offered us a day visit there, to have a look around the place and familiarise ourselves with the staff and surroundings. We would be picked up and returned home by ambulance. I could go with him and we would be offered aromatherapy and massages. Hubby agreed to this idea and our visitor kindly said she would arrange it all for us and be back in touch with a day visit appointment. Sadly time ran out and we never got our pre visit, guess it was just not to be. Now we would be going somewhere unfamiliar, if he did go in there to spend his last days.

After much family deliberation, plus support from both our community Macmillan Nurse and District Nurses, Mark elected to spend his last days in the Hospice. From the check list of notes we had written, it had far more positive points than the Hospital or Home and hardly any negative points at all and we really had looked into every eventuality. He needed far more support than we could cope with at home. The choice is a very individual thing, but for us it was the right one. The only thing worrying us was that we had never been to the Hospice before, making it unknown territory. But we knew that here he would be wonderfully cared for and I could be constantly by his side, so the decision was made. Our Macmillan Nurse rang in to book him a bed. She emphasised that the bed was the only one available at that time and we had to make an immediate decision to accept it or risk losing a place at the hospice altogether.

Everything was booked for his admittance the next morning. An Ambulance was arranged to pick us up for our journey to the Hospice. We were told to be ready for 8.30 am, but if they hadn't arrived for us by 12.00 noon, we were to ring in to the Hospice to let them know. Then they would chase them up.

The following morning, after a very unsettled night, and what was to be Mark's last night in his own home with all the emotions attached to that, we were up, about and ready early. Both feeling incredibly nervous, we were painfully aware that this would be his last trip anywhere, so anxious was definitely an understatement. The fact we had not already seen the Hospice for a pre visit was now looming big in my mind too.

Hubby was struggling terribly with his breathing by now and had started to use his emergency oxygen cylinder. He had learnt he could turn the pressure up higher on this by default, giving him more oxygen than he was prescribed. Although I felt this was wrong, I couldn't bring myself to take it off him, or lower the pressure. He was having dreadful panic attacks, unable to breathe properly, so I couldn't afford to add to his distress in any way, to do so would be cruel and so unfair at this late stage. If it helped him, I let him do it. I would tell the ambulance crew when they arrived and see what they said.

I was really hoping they wouldn't be late to pick us up, as the waiting was torture. I found myself pacing up and down the hall. I was constantly peering out of the window at anything that remotely sounded like a vehicle arriving in the street. All the time willing them to hurry up. Hubby was getting impatient, asking " how long now?!" 12.00 noon came and went, with no sign of them, it seemed a lifetime. I phoned the Hospice to let them know we were still at home, waiting for them. They said they would now chase it up.

Hubby looked so desperately ill, I wondered if he would cope with the wait much longer. Ashen, gasping for breath and panicking wasn't a good combination. I sat with him holding his hand, talking quietly to him, getting him to slow his breathing and calming him down.

The Ambulance arrived at 1.30 pm, meaning we had been waiting for it for 5 hours. But it was Hospital transport and they have to get people to appointments on time, so just one of those things. By now Hubby could not be moved easily, as he was so Ill. It took another 30 minutes to get him stable enough to move him into a wheelchair and into the Ambulance. I told them he was using the emergency cylinder of oxygen and had turned it up higher, but they said that was fine. They could see how poorly he was and were very patient and caring with him.

Finally we were gently settled into the Ambulance and on our way. The crew member sat with Hubby, keeping him calm by watching over him and talking to him continually. The journey seemed to take ages, but I think it was more about how I was feeling than reality. I stared out of the window, watching the traffic and pedestrians, people going about their daily business. I was suddenly jealous of their 'normal ' lives. How could they be carrying on routinely? Somehow it seemed disrespectful, shouldn't they be slowing down and showing sympathy for our plight? But of course they had no idea of what we were going through, where we were going, or why.

Lara

Where someone decides to die can be down to many, many different factors but there is one thing that is definite in my opinion; as far as is possible it should be the choice of the person who is dying. Of course it isn't always possible to carry out the wish of your loved one, death can come suddenly or unexpectedly, but Nick was able to have his wish.

The three main options were the three Hs; hospital, home or hospice. From the start he was definite, he did not want to die in a hospital. He had spent so much time in them over the years of his illness and, however kind and wonderful the staff had been, hospitals were not a place of peace or comfort for Nick. By necessity they were clinical in nature, they could be noisy, hospitals even have a certain smell about them, and staff could be over busy and rushed. I read a number of posts on Macmillan's site where people had died in hospital. Most were as positive an experience as can be, but it wasn't what Nick wanted so we ruled it out. That left two choices, home or hospice.

What mattered most to Nick at end of life was peace and calm, as much dignity as possible, to have his loved ones close and to be pain free. He chose the hospice so that I could be with him without doing any of the physical caring for him, husband and wife again not patient and carer, and also to have pain relief management immediately he needed it rather than maybe having to wait at home for a nurse or doctor to reach him. He had been in considerable pain and wanted to be as comfortable as possible so that he could concentrate on family, mattered hugely to him.

He knew the hospice as he had been going to breathlessness classes there and I had seen their counsellor once or twice. The atmosphere there was calm, gentle, comforting and surprisingly positive.

There were reasons Nick decided that dying at home wasn't what he wanted and those reasons partly related to him thinking of other people. So like him to still be thinking of others but in the end I think he made the right choice for the best of reasons. Of course we were fortunate that a bed was available when he needed it and that the hospital arranged for him to move there. Hospice beds are very limited and all hospices are charity run. It seems wrong that these centres of excellence for palliative care rely on hand outs.

Things we considered

Home
Pros
- Familiar surroundings
- Friends and family around familiar voices
- Comfortable
- Privacy

Cons
- How much support you have and how much time alone for the carer
- Unwanted visitors can be hard to manage
- Huge responsibility and not feeling able to cope with the nursing required
- How would I feel if he died when we were alone in the house
- No macmillan support at the weekend and evenings

Hospital
Pros
- Palliative care team and may know some of the staff
- Structured visiting hours can stop unwanted visitors

Cons
- No macmillan support at weekends and evenings
- Busy wards
- Hours of waiting around with little or no feedback
- Lack of emotional support
- Clinical and cold
- Lack of privacy

Hospice
Pros
- Expert at control of symptoms and pain relief
- Emotional Support
- Relaxed visiting times
- Good ratio staff around the clock
- Therapies available
- Compassionate and kind

Cons
- May be unknown territory
- Less clinical but still not familiar or "home"
- There are a limited number of hospices so may have to travel a considerable distance
- There may not be a bed available when needed

At the Hospice

Suzanna

We pulled into the grounds of the Hospice. It was a beautiful place, set in large rambling, well-kept gardens. The entire place had a serene, peaceful and calming atmosphere about it. Some patients had been wheeled into the grounds, complete with their beds, to take in some of the September Indian Summer sunshine and enjoy the beauty of the gardens.

On our arrival three Nurses came out to the Ambulance to meet and greet Mark and me. We were warmly welcomed, made to feel important and at ease. We were escorted inside and immediately I sensed a feeling of tranquillity all around us that is hard to describe. I knew instantly that this was where we were meant to be.

Each patient had their own private space, sectioned off from other patients, creating complete privacy. The sun shone in through the windows, beaming onto a reclining electric chair, it was light and airy in there, not at all cramped. In fact it had a lovely homely feel to it. There was a television to watch. A large wardrobe was available for both of our clothes, which I unpacked and hung up neatly. We were settled in and I was shown the bathroom and shower room available for my use.

The young Doctor soon appeared to come and see Mark. She talked to us for a while, asking questions, did some adjustments to his medications and checked him over. We had cancelled all further treatment and scans at the Hospital, he was too ill to be moved. It was just about keeping him pain free and comfortable now. We had both got a massage booked for 10am the next morning, to help relax us.

Mark was brought a meal but he couldn't face it, he did manage to eat his pudding though. He was very wobbly and shaky, yet he refused to get into bed. He sat in his wheelchair until the Nurses came and insisted he got into bed. They helped get him in and made sure he was comfortable and we settled down for the night. I had promised Hubby I would stay by his side, so I was given bedding and I snuggled into the reclining chair beside him.

Our Sons had visited earlier and had asked the Nurses to keep an eye on us, as we weren't the type of people to make a fuss or ask for help easily. A Nurse popped in, smiling, telling me she was doing what our Son's had asked. She brought me a hot chocolate and some toast, as she knew I hadn't eaten. She commented on how lovely and caring our Sons were, I had to smile to myself at their efforts to look out for us.

Mark actually had the best sleep in ages that night, with the help of altered meds and a ripple bed, he slept soundly. I just sat staring at him, thinking how sad it was that we were now at this final stage. I couldn't take my eyes off him, sleeping peacefully. I was so glad to see him looking relaxed and comfortable, for a change. I was perfectly happy to just sit by his side and watch over him all night long.

After a really relaxed night at the Hospice for Hubby and a cat nap for me, he woke up with a start. He was having a panic attack as he really was struggling to breathe now. I pressed the call button for the Nurses, but they were already on their way to him, with his early morning medication. They medicated him, calmed and settled him back down at roughly 7.30 am. They had just gone to move on to on to the next patient, when Mark started fitting. I immediately called them back, they asked me if he had done this before. I said yes but not as violently.

They came to his side and told me to talk to him as he could still hear me, I held his hand and spoke to him gently. With his free hand fisted, he suddenly clutched his chest and whoosh he was gone, as fast as that. It took us all by surprise, he had only been at the hospice for one night and now he was gone! As he had a DNR order active, he was allowed to slip, quietly and peacefully away.

There had been no time to alert family members and absolutely no chance of them getting there in time. So they had to be contacted and asked to come. But I was there, by his side and holding his hand, as promised. That was really lucky, because I was just about to go and take a shower before our massages. If I had gone, he would have been alone and maybe unnoticed.

Shortly afterwards, the whole family appeared at the Hospice, devastated and heartbroken at the news. Those that wanted to go and see him, to say goodbye, did, those that wanted to remember him as he was did so too. There was no pressure either way, it was all their own individual choices to make.

Our wonderful Husband / Father / Grandad / Twin Brother had now gone. He was out of his suffering and at peace. We were given a relatives room to use, while they sorted the formalities out. That room was warm and a little cramped and we were in there for quite some time. I was deeply shocked and sobbing, as were the whole family. We hugged each other in turn to give ourselves some comfort and support.

The patio doors of the room were open, to let some air in and we were spilling out onto the path outside. There were ten of us squashed into a small space, so more than a little tight. Suddenly a little robin appeared at the open doors, hopping about chirping for a while. We took that as a sign of comfort and were all amazed at his timely visit. Then he was gone just as quickly, a fleeting call to show himself at a very sad and traumatic time.

We drank copious amounts of tea and waited for all the necessary paperwork. The Nurses popped in and out to check how we were doing and suggested we called our GP out, as I was in shock. Although we knew it was coming towards the end of Mark's life, I don't think anyone actually believed it would happen that soon or that suddenly.

Everyone had been so kind and the shortness of our stay did not detract from the importance of being there. We were treated with respect and Hubby had been given the peace and dignity deserved by such a private and gentle man. It gave him comfort and relief from pain in his final hours, for which we will always be grateful.

I knew having me by his side as he slipped away had provided him with his last wish and allowed me to fulfil my promise to him, to stay beside him and hold his hand. It would have been so different if I had taken that shower.

Our Sons had asked if they could stay a little later the night before, but were told only if death was imminent. How ironic that death, had indeed been incredibly close.
But things happen that way sometimes, it's so unpredictable, just one of those things. Maybe that was the way Hubby would have liked it.

Sometimes the patients loved one has just left the room and the patient dies, depriving them of being there at their final moment. There was a lady on the Macmillan community site, who had just popped to the toilet, her Husband had passed away when she got back to him. She felt absolutely dreadful about it. But another member said not to feel bad, maybe he had just followed her out of the room? What a wonderful and comforting thought. This is how I would like to have thought it happened, if that had sadly happened to me.

Her Husband would have known she was around and he just slipped away as she slipped out of the room. Our Sons couldn't be there as their Dad slipped away, but he knew they had all been there for him and had visited frequently throughout his illness. The same for his Twin Sister, it just wasn't possible for any of them to get to him in an instance. No regrets, no guilt. They all loved him and he knew it. At the end of the day that was all that mattered. Every one of them came rushing to the Hospice, when they were called. United in grief, but there for each other, as it should be.

Lara

When Nick arrived at the hospice I will never forget how his face and whole body just seemed to relax. I think he knew that he was somewhere safe, somewhere that he would be pain free. The calm, quiet atmosphere of his room, which looked out onto a beautiful garden, gave him some peace. It was as if then and there he made the decision to let nature take its course and let go of life. The two to three months turned out to be less than two weeks.

Nick had been in the hospice for a few nights and I had gone home to get a few hours better sleep. I was woken at about 7am by my mobile. One of the hospice nurses gently told me that Nick's breathing was changing and she thought I should get to the Hospice as soon as I could. For some reason I told her I would be there as soon as I had got hold of our son at University and helped him find a way home quickly. I went and told our other son, who was getting ready for work ,and he called the office straight away to let them know he wouldn't be in, I then got on the phone.

I couldn't get hold of our son, his hall at University was concrete built and reception was awful. I was in a bit of a panic by this time but still hadn't headed to the hospice and the nurse called again telling me gently that I needed to come straight away. I think in a way I just wasn't ready to accept this was the end, so soon after Nick had stopped treatment and when we were still supposed to have a couple of months together. But cancer doesn't work like that. I felt guilt about the delay for a long time.

I asked my sister to get our son home saying tell him to get a taxi, that will be quickest, and headed off to the hospice with our other son after quickly letting Nick's brother know and telling him to tell the rest of Nick's family. My parents were staying at our house so they knew.

At the hospice we found Nick weak and quiet but still conscious. Our son arrived and then my sister and one of Nick's brother and we spent the day in his room talking with him. His parent's didn't come, I think it was too much for them and that is fine. He was still trying to keep us at ease with his dry sense of humour, how he did that I don't know. He had time with everyone alone and the day passed with us giving each other support and strength. There was so much love in that peaceful room that day.

I believe Nick didn't want our son's distress to be more than need be and at about 6pm he encouraged them to go home, to get some food and to rest. I told them they should do what felt right, they could say their goodbyes or they could come back at any stage, that they could stay if they wanted. In the end they left after final words with their beloved father, a hug and a kiss. It was too much for them and for Nick and I understand and respect that. His brother had already gone and my sister promised to come back after seeing all was okay at home.

To be honest I was grateful to have a little time with my husband on my own but I know he had asked my sister to be here for me at the end of his life. After about twenty minutes the nurse let me know someone had arrived to see Nick. It was the friend who had been the hugest support and I didn't feel I could deny him the right to say goodbye so in he came. He talked with Nick and I could see that he was feeling very emotional but also that Nick was now very, very weak. After what felt like an age but was probably an hour I told him I needed time alone with Nick and saw him out. I came back and held Nick's hand as he lay quietly listening to some soft music. At one point he gestured for me to come close and as I put my head close he whispered in my ear "I love you". That was the last thing he ever said. I hope he heard my reply.

The hospice nurses came quietly in and out of the room, checking on him and me and my sister when she returned. By now he was unresponsive to anything but the nurses care still continued. When he became restless they gave him a boost of medication and he became peaceful again. They brought in a glass with some solution in it and a small sponge on a stick so I could moisten his mouth and lips. They offered me warm drinks as I sat next to him all night, although I rarely accepted, as my sister rested on a pull up bed they bought for her. She left us together while letting me feel she was near which was just right. The tears rolled down my cheeks that night as I whispered quietly to my darling man.

There was one thing I so wanted to do but couldn't. I couldn't lie down next to Nick and hold him close as he left this world. As it was I sat next to him and gently held his hand and stroked his hair, talking quietly to him, with my sister holding his other hand. The hospice nurses had been quietly checking on us and him, would have stayed if that was what we wanted, and explained what was happening and answered all my questions honestly and kindly. I wasn't able to hold him but I was supported and he was peaceful and that in the end I suppose is what mattered most.

By early morning Nick's breathing was becoming much slower and I could sense that he had not got long left to live. I went and got a nurse and she confirmed that it wouldn't be long. I held his hand and stroked his hair and talked quietly to him, trying to keep as calm as I could and not break the peace that was in the room. My sister asked if she could sit and hold his other hand. I said yes, he would have liked that and maybe he knew. The nurse asked if we wanted her to stay and I said yes please. She was a quiet comfort behind me with her hand on my shoulder. Nick's breathing just slowed down and down until the next breath didn't come.

As soon as I felt able I phoned our sons. One decided to come to the hospice and the other not. He wanted to remember his dad alive and that was fine. There is no right or wrong in this situation as far as I am concerned and he had said his goodbyes. The other came in to see his dad to give him a final kiss.

Nick was no longer in pain, no longer suffering. He had gone and become a past tense, a memory. But he was still with us;

in the boys genes, in all the life lessons he taught us and in all we shared. He still is.

Feelings after Death

Suzanna's Sorry

I tried to visit my feelings shortly after Hubby died, but I simply felt numb and sometimes desperately lonely, even in a crowded room and especially amongst couples. I miss Hubby terribly, our relationship, companionship, our partnership, the hugs, especially the hugs and I crave them like never before. I am a tactile person, I need my hugs.

I can cope on my own, sometimes I like my own company and my independence. I can come and go as I please, changing plans and direction at the drop of a hat, without having to let anyone know. But that doesn't mean I am happy with my situation. It just means I am coping with life as it is now.

I find I make friends quite easily, but as my situation changes, so does my group of friends. I feel you gravitate towards people at the same stage and situation as you are at in life. Only someone who has actually been through the same experience as you have, can truly understand your mind set and where you are at emotionally. This is what makes my friendship with Lara so very precious and important to me, she really 'gets ' it 100%.

I have changed, as have my values, interests and needs, it is simply not possible for me to remain the same person I was before Hubby's death. That person left when he died, gone forever, replaced by a tougher, no nonsense personality. I feel closer to people that have been in my life at a very vulnerable, personal and emotional time. People that were there for me when I needed them , helped me enormously , travelled my journey with me and supported me unconditionally and continually , hence the bond I formed with our Hospital Macmillan Nurse . I have friends that have done just that too, I also have friends that have run for the hills!

My way of coping at the moment, is to keep looking forwards, not looking backwards or sideways. I guess almost like wearing blinkers. Looking straight ahead, to the future and all this new and changed life may hold.

I do not feel bitter about everything that has happened, very sad maybe. But as Hubby would say "it is what it is, that's life, ". I have never been a person to carry grudges , hatred , envy , bitterness, spite , ill feelings , greed , malice or anger and I'm not a ' woe is me ' type either . It's not to say that all of these feelings have not touched me at some point, it's just that I don't carry them on. I have learnt to handle my emotions, deal with them and then let them go. Holding on to them is only harmful to myself, my health and wellbeing. So let them go and be free of them, it's not a nice burden to carry.

I have never been materialistic either and never wished to hurt anyone. I believe in fate, that when your time is up, it's up. There is absolutely nothing that can be done to change that. Because we are born when we are meant to be born and we die when we are meant to die. It's as simple as that in my eyes. You can't control life in any way, you have to accept it and carry on to the best of your ability. You get the hand of cards that life has dealt you. I feel that thinking like this has helped me enormously to cope and to come to terms with my 'lot' in life. It isn't always fair, but that's just the way it happens.

I also try to think about what would have happened if I had died first, leaving Hubby behind. How would he have coped without me? I would like to think he would carry on taking care of our children and Grandchildren. I feel he would be proud of me for plodding on, tackling things I have never done before because I need to. I will carry on and strive to keep his memory alive for our family and the generation to come, as the circle of life continues on.

Lara

Once the funeral was over everyone started to get back to their normal lives. Everyone except immediate family and one very dear friend of Nick's who took his death particularly hard. When I visited my in-laws Nick's name wasn't mentioned and if I talked about him there was no response, the subject was just changed. That was how they coped. On a recent visit my mother-in-law mentioned Nick for the first time since he died and how she dreams about him. I needed to hear her say that.

There was no getting back to normal in our home. I'm not sure any of us really knew what "normal" was. There was this huge hole in our hearts and in our lives that had been filled by Nick and it was like we were restarting not resuming. One of our sons had sat his GCSEs very soon after Nick's diagnosis and had to sit his degree finals very shortly after his death. Our other son had gone through University and started his first big job. They had a lot of adjusting to do on top of grieving after having so much extra pressure at such key times in their lives. Although they no longer worried about their dad they felt his absence strongly and started worrying more about me.

For quite some time I simply existed. I struggled to be away from the house for any time. The first time I stayed away for a night I left early the next morning simply because I needed to get back to the security of home. Nothing felt right or "normal" and suddenly I had so much time on my hands I didn't know what to do with myself or where to start with all the jobs and paperwork that needed doing. So many people needed informing of Nick's death, so many forms needed filling in and accounts changing to my name.

I remember one day I was put through to the bereavement team to get a particular direct debit put in my name. Once all the formalities had been gone through the young man on the end of the phone asked for my details for the direct debit. On receiving my title and name he interrupted me. "But you're not a Mrs are you? Not anymore. You're a Ms now". His insensitivity hit me far more than his lack of knowledge. I told him, far more calmly than I felt, that I was indeed still a Mrs and after felt low for the rest of the day. That wasn't the only insensitivity I met at the end of the phone, although I also spoke to some really lovely helpful people who had just the perfect tone to their voice and dealt with my queries quickly, efficiently and calmly. Getting up in the morning and getting through the day was doable, finding the incentive to do anything productive was less easy.

Small steps. I took small steps forwards, backwards and sideways. It felt like I was travelling through an endless maze, occasionally crossing paths with strangers and old friends, new experiences; good, bad, happy and sad. Old friends who had become strangers while Nick was ill jumped out of the hedges at me and acted as if the last five years just hadn't existed. I was supposed to be the same, just without Nick. New friends came along and lead me through some of the trickier parts of the labyrinth. Old friends who had been there throughout turned up when I needed them most. And so I just kept going, despite the emptiness that was inside me much of the time, because that is what we do and if I didn't then the cancer would have succeeded in taking even more.

Grief

Suzanna

Grief comes in waves and in varying degrees of waves at that. From the great big tidal waves that are bigger than you, they come crashing ashore, engulfing you and knocking you right off your feet, leaving you running for safety. Right down to the gentle waves that lap your toes and allow you to paddle and feel the loss, but still cope with it. There can be a massive time lapse to get from the giant waves down to the smaller ones.

When Mark died I believe I hit the floor running, talk about fight or flight mode. Running seemed to be my only option, even if toned down to continually being on the move. This was my defence mechanism. If I filled all of my hours and kept active I wasn't allowing time to dwell on the situation and go into a downhill spiral of grief and deep despair ~ for me it worked. But was I just running from the truth, refusing to face the enormity of losing my life partner. Some days I can feel okay to carry on, others I'm overcome with grief that leaves me feeling hopeless and lost, overpowered by my emotions.

There are the stages that grief takes you through, ranging from denial, anger , disbelief , deep sorrow , bitterness , looking for someone to blame, emptiness, loneliness and a yearning for the return of your loved one. You don't sleep as your mind is in turmoil, you don't eat or you comfort eat, depending on your reaction to your grief. You can feel very numb for quite some time, which I think is nature's way of protecting you from your pain. You cry, or you don't cry, this depends a lot on personality. There is no time limit to grieving, it has to run its course , it can't be rushed or skipped over in any way , it just has to be felt and dealt with as best you can .

Healing comes with time and support and not pushing yourself. Everyone is different, handling things in different ways. Some people wish to talk it through, others don't, and you just have to go with whatever helps you as an individual. The support is out there for those who need it and it comes in many shapes, it can be through talking to friends and family, counselling, medications, your religion, support groups, remembering your loved one, raising funds in their memory. Planting a tree or a rose bush, putting a plaque on a bench, so many options. There is no time limit to grief, you will always carry your loved one in your heart and have happy memories that are yours alone to keep and no one can ever take them away from you , remember that and let it bring you comfort.

For me, I think grieving was delayed by the feeling of complete numbness, as initially I spent my time sorting out the practicalities. The funeral and the endless paperwork that followed seemed to take up all of my time and energy. I seemed to hit the floor running and went into automatic pilot. My children took it in turns to stay with me in the early days, as bless them, they didn't want to leave me alone. So I guess I was cocooned and protected from the enormity of it all for a while. It actually took several sessions of counselling to help me slowly face my grief and I then went through the whole range of feelings.

I feel I still use the tactic of running away up to this very day, filling my days and my mind to navigate away from my pain. I guess I'm now at the paddle and feel it, yet cope stage, but it has taken me time to get here. I'm not feeling the full force of my grief and I don't allow it to rule me or engulf me, rightly or wrongly this is how I cope. The sheer will to carry on has kept me going, my family and friends give me the reason and my desire to write about what Hubby went through and coped with has given me the strength. I'm still grieving , I will always miss Hubby , I miss being a Wife , someone's other half ,part of a couple, but I am still a Mom and a Nanny , so life goes on .

Lara

I have experienced grief before, when my dearest friend died from cancer a few years before Nick did. I couldn't control the tears, they would strike anywhere and anytime, in the supermarket, the car, talking to someone about something totally unrelated, taking a mouthful of food... The grief was raw, painful, exhausting and thoughts of her were constantly in my head.

When Nick died I reacted very differently. Hardly shedding a tear, hardly thinking about him, I felt no real emotions. Apart from a lump in my throat when our sons stood up at the funeral to honour their dad I felt nothing that day. I wandered around the wake afterwards, with a glass of water in my hand, talking to the people from all walks of his life who were there telling me about their memories of my husband and I smiled at them as they spoke about him and laughed when they told me something funny .

This continued for several months. I just got on with life. If Nick did pop into my thoughts all I saw was him dead in the hospice, nothing else, so I blocked it out. I would make myself talk with our sons about him on occasion and listen to them talking about him but it was out of duty nothing more. I wanted to cry, I wanted to scream at the top of my voice and throw things but I was unable to. Previously the tissues would have been out watching a moving film but I could look at the screen dry eyed. I felt lost in an emotionless bubble.

I had always been a heart over head kind of person and couldn't understand why I was behaving this way or why I had grieved more for a friend than my life partner. So I took myself off to a counsellor once again to see if she could help me. I told her how I was behaving and that I desperately wanted to feel the grief I knew must be there but that I was unable to.

To cut a long story short I am still seeing her and only recently have I started feeling again. Grief comes sporadically, without warning, and can be as raw and painful as if I had only just lost Nick. She believes I was suffering from PTS and maybe she was right. It was like I was unable to deal with what we had been through for the previous five years and so my brain shut down its emotional side until I was able to start coping with grief and let me grieve at a rate that I could cope with.

I have cried, and screamed and broken a few things. I forget birthdays and I double book appointments. I have had days when the only reason I got out of bed was because my dog needed a walk and some food. I have felt unable to be away from the safety of my home for more than a few hours, now a few days, and I have filled every moment from dawn to dusk with unimportant and often unnecessary jobs just to block out an isolated weekend. I have felt my loneliest when in company, for example sitting around the kitchen table with friends from our student days, and desperately sad watching my parents sit on the sofa holding hands as they watch a favourite television programme.

I don't know how long I will grieve for Nick, probably for always as I had never imagined a life without him. But as time passes I am sure it will change and become more bearable, I will remember the good memories more than the bad or sad ones. I talk to him still but it is already changing from asking him questions he can't answer and regretting that he isn't there to share some thing with, to telling him about something I have achieved on my own or something about family and friends, especially our boys. He told me I'd need to push myself outside my comfort zone to build a new life and every time I do that I tell him and hope he would be proud of me or at least pleased that I did, after all, listen to his advice.

Moving On

Suzanna

Although life will never be the same, or the life we planned, it still goes on. 'Time and Tide waits for no man '. I plan to leave behind happy memories, some monetary gifts, a book, plus personalised letters for all of my family, now is the time to start work on all of these things. I have the time and love to give, so now I want to leave my mark.

I am generally an upbeat, optimistic, glass half full type of person. But losing Hubby knocked me right off my feet, leaving me feeling lost, fallen and badly shaken. It has taken time to climb back up and start to feel like me again. Slowly I will get there, given the time and space I need to do so. Healing for me consists of keeping busy, helping others when and where I can and spending quality time with family and friends. I also find keeping a sense of humour is so important, seeing the funny side of life in all eventualities is a coping strategy that I find important and helps me to stay grounded and upbeat.

Generally I find people don't want to hear doom and gloom and will gravitate towards happy go lucky people, to help them feel good. A good laugh can be a tonic , but life has its ups and downs and it can be very difficult to stay upbeat all the time , we all have down days , me included and never so many as just now . It's only natural that something as big as losing your life partner will have a massive impact on your life and emotional wellbeing.

I find writing very therapeutic, so this book has helped me some way along the healing path. I have a strong desire to help others in this situation. The fact that I've written with another ex-carer who has travelled this journey with me in a parallel world, makes it so much more special to me. I will continue to fundraise for Macmillan and try to support people along the way too. Helping people is also self-healing in a deep spiritual way, you don't have to be religious to be spiritual and feel it either. It gives you a warm, contented feeling of satisfaction, it's so rewarding to think you may have helped somebody else on this same awful journey.

Just when I think I'm coping really well something can set me right back. It doesn't have to be a big issue, something small can trip me up and send me spiralling down. Something breaking or something I can't find, a missed appointment, forgetting someone's Birthday. Feeling incompetent in any way or not completely in control can spin my head, setting me into a panic. I start to wonder if I'm coping as well as I should be, or as I think I am.

Recently in the middle of the night, I discovered there was a missed item from the prescription bag I had just collected, this sent me into a panic. I didn't know if I hadn't ordered it, the Doctors had missed it off, or the chemist hadn't given it to me by mistake and I spent all night mithering over it, who should I ring first, the chemist or the Doctors? . Mulling it over and over in my head, I tried to reason that if I had forgotten to order it, I could reorder, but what if they said I had already had it? As it was anti-depressants, would I come crashing down without them? I had several hours to wait for the chemist to open, so why couldn't I just sleep and sort it out when I woke up? Because in the middle of the night it is a big issue, everything seems magnified and once I'm awake I struggle to get back to sleep, especially if I have any sort of problem on my mind. I believe I swallow my grief down and it escapes in other areas, such as panicking over things that could be easily sorted out.

Sleeping can be a big problem for lots of bereaved people, there is so much on your mind and night time seems to bring it all to the forefront. There is something about four in the morning, I seem to have an alarm clock for that time. Once awake the chances of getting back to sleep are very slim. Then when it's actually time to get up I feel ready to drop off, it's so frustrating. When I have a worry on my mind I can never rest until it's sorted and I have an answer to my problem. As I no longer have Hubby to share my worries with, I need to learn to calm myself down. Hubby was wonderful at solving my problems and worries for me, he seemed to have a solution for everything. I miss his calm reasoning enormously.

Initially I couldn't even think of tackling any practical tasks. But Mark had started to gut our kitchen, to bring it up to date with new units, new flooring, re plastering in parts and redecorating. He also wanted to take off some old artex from the ceiling. But the stretching up pulled his back and he developed sciatica which took him right off his feet. With hindsight, we believe this was the first sign of his illness. He never returned to good health after that episode.

Obviously the decorating was abandoned at this stage, leaving unfinished plastering and a bare concrete floor, which was very cold and dusty. It was left like this for some time. When Hubby was rushed into Hospital with pulmonary embolisms, I took the decision to get someone in to at least cover the floor with laminate tiling.

I knew Mark would be annoyed at this, as he wanted to do it all himself, But as we were having to have district nurses in daily, a concrete floor would be difficult to keep clean or mop. So I decided now was the perfect time to get it laid down properly and at least it would be one less job for Hubby to worry about. He did complain, but I think secretly he was glad it had been done. It was so much more hygienic and suitable for a cancer patient.

Mark kept saying he would start work on the new kitchen again as soon as he was better, bless him. Deep down I knew this wouldn't happen , as he would never be well enough to start work on it again , But I just went along with him saying , yes that will be good , so not to upset him .

When Mark died the kitchen stood still for a while, bare walls staring at me daily. The following summer I decided enough was enough and arranged to have it done whilst I was away on holiday, with a close friend. As it was being done by a family member and his work mate, I had no worries about having strangers in my house and happily left my keys with him. If I'm honest it meant I didn't have to watch someone else complete a project that was Mark's.

I wanted shiny white units with grey work tops and tiles. Mark would have been happy with that, as we had already decided on those colours. We had always clashed over colour schemes when it came to decorating. It was as if we never liked each other's tastes. So it always took us ages to decide on a new colour theme, we usually ended up compromising. When the kitchen fitters arrived with the paint colours charts for the walls, I simply wanted white walls. They laughed saying, there was no point bringing the charts then. I laughed too, but inside I was thinking, would Hubby have wanted plain white walls? Well probably not, but I did and I ended up so pleased with my choice. It was light and airy and easily wipeable if the Grandchildren touched the walls with grubby hands, leaving fingerprints and handprints.

I emptied all the cupboards before I went away, upon my return, it was all done. Brilliant idea, I had been away from the mess, painting and plastering. The kitchen was now looking brand new and very beautiful indeed.

The taxi driver who picked us up from the airport offered to carry my bags in for me, as they were heavy. When he saw the kitchen he said " wow, I like your kitchen, to which I replied "wow, so do I!". He looked at me as if I was crazy. But once I explained it had all been newly done whilst I was away, the penny dropped and he realised I was seeing it for the first time too!

I'm sure Hubby would have approved of the new kitchen, he wouldn't want me to continually live in a mess of a half done kitchen. It needed to be finished. Once one project was tackled I felt more able to tackle other jobs that needed doing.

Everything I experienced during my time as a wife who became a carer has been a massive learning curve. I feel you learn something from, and carry a small piece of, each and every person you meet and spend considerable time with.
 The lessons learnt, for me have been enormous, the biggest one being from my wonderful husband. His bravery, dignity, perseverance, attitude and sheer grit throughout his illness were truly astounding. He taught me so much about coping alone, as he and he alone could fight against his cancer. As much as you try to share their illness and support them through it, it is actually theirs alone to cope with. In the same way as living without them, when they die is yours alone to cope with.
 More lessons have been learnt from the reactions of others to Hubby's illness and death. The Nurses that take care of

dying people daily are very special people and have taught me lots about compassion and caring. My counsellor taught me valuable coping alone strategies. I was never bothered about people knowing I was having counselling, to me it was never a secret. I was watching my wonderful Hubby die before my very eyes, of course I would need counselling. My family and friends have confirmed the importance of pulling together in times of crisis, by rallying round and supporting us. I also learnt that asking for help is not a weakness, but a strength, as admitting you are not coping alone takes courage.

My wonderful writing partner, a dear and trusted friend, has been a big help towards my coping, by just being there and making me feel I am not alone. The fact we are coping together side by side has been an enormous comfort. My best friend , who I spend leisure time with , shop , walk , chat, laugh , cry , confide in and holiday with has got me through some very tough times . I will always be grateful to all these people for helping me to cope now I am alone.

The friends I lost along the way taught me that not everyone can cope with it all. It's massive and sends shockwaves and ripples outwards that touch and affect others, sometimes driving people away. I am sad about that , but after Mark's death , for a while I became high maintenance , lashing out and hurting people unintentionally , as I was hurting deeply , struggling to cope and not doing too well at it , despite my attempts of pretending otherwise .

Now I am much stronger, I'm a survivor and am coping alone, to the best of my ability. Hopefully I will continue to improve slowly over time. I have learnt how to run our home alone, fixing things I would never have attempted to do before, taking over every practical task I can reasonably handle. It is going to take time, but I am heading towards coping alone slowly yet surely.

Lara

Life is very different now. I still grieve for Nick but slowly, bit by bit, I am starting to build a life without him. It has taken time even to contemplate a life alone, but the human instinct to live is strong and I decided I couldn't spend the rest of my time just existing.

So I am trying new things and learning a lot, about myself as well as other things. I am more capable than I imagined and braver too. I can now walk into a room full of strangers without my heart beating so hard and fast I fear it can be seen, I can spend time alone not always longing for company. I can get on a plane and go to new places without Nick by my side and I have new hobbies which I wish I'd discovered years ago. I am kinder to myself.

When I feel lonely it is a special kind of loneliness. I don't necessarily want someone to go out on a long walk with or for a meal or to the cinema, but I miss the someone to do nothing with, the someone who knows me better than I know myself to share my thoughts with and the someone who makes me feel totally at ease and relaxed.

There is so much to miss. His laugh, his teasing, his kindness and his intelligence. His logical way of sorting something out, and his soft voice that was never raised. His love. But there is also so much to remember and so much I learnt from him. I ask myself what Nick would say if I am stuck with making a decision or how we would cope with a situation together and how I can adapt that to do it alone. I see him in our children all the time and that makes me smile as does knowing how proud he would be of the kind, considerate and fun adults they have become. I hope he'd be proud of me too. I still talk to him in my head and share things with him. Occasionally I'll have a few words with him for leaving me behind, but mostly the one-sided conversations are gentle and comforting.

Hopefully, one of my courses or new hobbies, or both, will lead to me finding a new, self-employed job. I have changed and the things I used to do don't feel right for me anymore. I want to do things that I enjoy, give me pleasure and make me feel useful, we all need a purpose in life. But my priorities have changed, I tend not to put things off anymore, I am still quite an impulsive person but am learning that a bit of planning isn't a bad thing. Enjoyment matters and a bit of risk taking doesn't hurt either. Family remain a top priority for me but I try to look after myself a bit better too.
Life goes on, for as long as it does, and I need to make more memories of my own.

The Circle of Life

Suzanna

The circle of life moves on and has seen two new and very precious additions to our ever growing family. Our very first, and very beautiful, Granddaughter appeared almost twelve months after Mark's death. Finally after four Sons, followed by four Grandsons, a little girl joined the family. An unexpected female, it was almost as if Hubby had sent her along as a wonderful parting gift. She became the youngest member of our family.

But not for long, as our fifth and incredibly handsome Grandson arrived six months later. I am very touched to say that he has his Grandad's Christian name as a middle name. Taking his name on ensures that it will be carried on into the next generation of our family. This is a lovely tribute to Hubby, but it is so sad to think that the two new arrivals will never meet their Grandad, or that he will never see them or play a part in their lives.

My Sons and their partners have been incredibly supportive to me, through my grief and my journey into my now solo existence. My Grandchildren have been a massive comfort to me and I enjoy their company enormously, along with their unconditional love and the endless hugs and kisses they provide, they give me the will to carry on. I am sure Mark would have been very proud of all our grandchildren, and also of our sons and the men they have become.

I love every single member of my family dearly and my Grandchildren will always hold a very special place in my heart. They mean the world to me, keeping me young minded and grounded. Their boundless energy and zest for life, keeps me alert in both mind and body. They don't allow me any time to feel sorry for myself or to let my grief take me over.

I believe that Mark lives on, through his sons and grandchildren. As the circle of life continues on our family grows and renews itself, it's a fact of life and a natural process. I see different traits of Hubby in different family members, a genetic imprint destined to carry on. It's comforting and reassuring to see certain mannerisms of his appear at random times.

Lara

We may be a small family but I have been so lucky to have their love and support throughout Nick's illness and now after he has gone and while I try slowly to make a new life, a life I never imagined. Our sons have made me so proud since Nick's death and my only regret is that he isn't here to see them grow and develop as fine young men.

Of course they miss their dad but he lives on in them. I see so much of him in their mannerisms and attitudes and their human decency. Maybe, if they have children of their own one day (oh, I would like to be a gran so much. At the moment I just enjoy watching Suzanna's grow in the photos she sends me) they will have a bit of the grandad they will never meet in them. I hope so.

We were "lucky" to get extra years with Nick that no-one expected us to have. The circle was bigger than it was supposed to be for him, it's just a shame it couldn't have been bigger still.

Epilogue - Meeting Each other

Suzanna

My beautiful writing partner has been a constant bright star, shining throughout my darkest hours. For that I will never be able to pay her back , she has kept me calm through traumas , motivated throughout our writing , encouraged , guided , edited me . Helped me laugh when I need it, cry when I need it, kept me grounded at all times and all of this without even meeting each other! I don't think she realises how lovely she really is.

Needless to say meeting up would become essential at some point, to carry out work on our book together. Things like sequencing, adding, removing, altering, correcting, blending and editing would all demand decisions and time spent together. We hoped to meet up in the summer months, during the lighter, warmer days as it would involve a lengthy journey. We would then spend time trawling through the pages. As it was to be our initial introduction meet ' in the flesh ', a few hours to get to know each other would be best. Chatting online and meeting face to face are two entirely different situations, but we knew we would get along together just fine, we had been chatting together for more than two years since Hubby's diagnosis. We arranged to meet at my house.

I think we were both a little nervous and I wondered if I would come up to her expectations. Meeting Lara was every bit as wonderful as I had hoped and more. We hugged on sight, she was beautiful, friendly, and open. , honest and warm natured, why ever were we nervous? I felt at ease instantly and after minutes we were like old friends meeting up after a gap apart. We chatted, lunched, looked at our writing and got to know each other, it was a total delight to be in her presence. Hopefully we will meet up many more times on our writing journey. Lara you are a star.

Lara

It was a very strange concept, writing a book with someone I had never physically met.

Having met on an online forum where there was a group for people who cared for a loved one with cancer we became friends in a virtual world. I didn't understand how online friendship could work before I joined the group but they do. Because everyone in the group is both in a similar situation and anonymous it is easy to open up to them unlike anyone else. Anonymous but not without character or personality, both of those shine through the words they write and sometimes you just click with someone. Suzanna and I clicked.

Our friendship grew both online and through the private messages of support and friendship we sent to each other and I can honestly say that knowing Suzanna, even in a virtual world, helped me more than I can explain. Her kindness and her caring nature came through her words. She made me laugh, let me cry and soothed me with her calmness.

Writing without meeting worked. We were in constant contact electronically, Suzanna had the determination and drive to keep me on track and encourage me when I was lagging behind or doubting that I had anything useful to say. We knew so much about each other and each other's families, it got to the point where we not only needed to meet to talk through progress on the book but we also wanted to.

I was, I have to say, petrified. What if she didn't like me, what if we found each other completely different to the picture we had built up? I had no need to be nervous. As soon as that front door was opened and we gave each other a hug the nerves vanished. Suzanna's warmth and generous spirit filled her home and everything I had imagined about her was true, a real life Mrs Weasley. I owe her so much and I have made a very dear friend for life.

Printed in Great Britain
by Amazon